From Massacres
to Genocide

ROBERT I. ROTBERG
THOMAS G. WEISS
Editors

From
MASSACRES
to
GENOCIDE

*The Media, Public Policy, and
Humanitarian Crises*

THE BROOKINGS INSTITUTION
Washington, D.C.

THE WORLD PEACE FOUNDATION
Cambridge, Massachusetts

Copyright © 1996 by the World Peace Foundation
One Eliot Square, Cambridge, Massachusetts 02138-4952

The views expressed in this book are solely those of the editors and contributing authors and should not be ascribed to the trustees, officers, or
other staff members of the sponsoring institutions or of the Brookings
Institution.

Library of Congress Cataloging-in-Publication data

From massacres to genocide : the media, humanitarian crises, and
  policy-making / edited by Robert I. Rotberg and Thomas G. Weiss.
    p. cm.
  Includes bibliographical references and index.
  ISBN 0-8157-7590-3 (cloth). — ISBN 0-8157-7589-X (pbk.)
  1. Disaster relief. 2. International relief. 3. Disasters in the
press. 4. Mass media. 5. Public relations—Disaster relief.
6. Human rights. I. Rotberg, Robert I. II. Weiss, Thomas George.
HV553.F76 1996
363.3'4526—dc20   95-50159
                                                             CIP

9 8 7 6 5 4 3 2 1

The paper used in this publication meets the minimum requirements
of the American National Standard for Information Sciences—
Permanence of Paper for Printed Library Materials, ANSI Z39-48-1984.

Typeset in Times Roman

Composition by Linda Humphrey
Arlington, Virginia

Printed by R. R. Donnelley and Sons Co.
Harrisonburg, Virginia

Preface

LARGE-SCALE human suffering is a continuing threat to world peace. Each year several dozen gruesome civil wars disturb global order and jar our collective conscience. Recurrent ethnic and religious strife from Angola to Guatemala, unthinkable acts of inhumanity in Bosnia and Rwanda, and violence accompanying the unraveling of the former Soviet Union demonstrate that neighbors killing neighbors is a global reality with potentially ominous implications for the entire international community.

The 50 million people displaced by current complex humanitarian emergencies overwhelm the post-post–Cold War world's ability to understand and to cope with genocide, ethnic cleansing, massacres, and other inhumane acts. The United Nations and regional groups have tried, but they cannot successfully manage the proliferation of tragedies without greater public awareness of how much is at stake, and how much more expensive it is to act later rather than sooner.

The media play an increasingly crucial role in publicizing humanitarian crises, and advances in technology have intensified the immediacy of their reports. Because global communication networks facilitate intensive, ongoing coverage of crises throughout the world as they unfold, policy-makers are under great pressure to respond rapidly to events. Close cooperation between international relief agencies and the media is thus essential to help prevent and contain the complex humanitarian emergencies that threaten to overwhelm the world's capacity to assist and to care in the post-post–Cold War era.

If their efforts can be focused and sustained by collaboration with humanitarians, the media can decisively alter both public attitudes and the actions of policy-makers to the benefit of those who are menaced by life-threatening suffering. It is thus possible, along the lines suggested in the following pages, to augment the tensile strength of the international humanitarian safety net protecting suffering populations.

The World Peace Foundation and the Humanitarianism and War Project of Brown University's Thomas J. Watson Jr. Institute for International Studies joined forces to explore the interactions among the media, policy-makers, and humanitarians. Our working hypothesis was that future Bosnias, Rwandas, and Somalias can be avoided, as well as relieved, and that the media have a crucial contribution to make that goes well beyond the crudeness of what is termed the "CNN factor." At the same time, we were well aware that far more creative information-sharing among these groups is essential, not only because the American public and others around the world receive so much of their information about distant dilemmas from the media, but also because relief agencies seek to mobilize members of the media and influence decision-makers.

This book contains significantly redrafted versions of many of the papers prepared for a conclave organized in Cambridge, Massachusetts, in December 1994. We explored four major questions central to tensions among humanitarian agencies, policy-makers, and the media as they addressed crises:

—Given the episodic and capricious quality of news coverage of various humanitarian crises, what can and should be done to improve it?

—Is it possible to improve communications among the different actors to resolve or avoid major conflicts and benefit affected civilian populations?

—Can the media and humanitarian organizations provide information to policy-makers in a more timely and systematic fashion? Given distortions in the information conveyed, can the information provided to policy-makers be improved?

—To what extent and in what ways do breakthroughs in electronic technology offer new possibilities for wider international coverage of complex humanitarian emergencies, broadened public awareness of issues, and more appropriate policy-making and humanitarian responses?

One-third of the meeting participants were working journalists. The rest were drawn from public and private aid agencies, academia, and government. The workshop's deliberations were built around five sessions, each addressing specific issues through a series of commissioned papers. A sixth, concluding, session drew together themes and recommendations.

We thank the participants for their formative comments, Colin Scott for his assistance as rapporteur, and Larry Minear for his guidance in framing many of the issues. We are grateful to Ann Hannum for not only organizing the December meeting but also overseeing the timely production of this volume; neither would have occurred without her able help. We are also grateful to the Pew Charitable Trusts for financial support to the Humanitarianism and War Project, which in turn made possible the Watson Institute's cosponsorship of our meeting.

R. I. R.
T. G. W.
August 1995

Contents

Part Two—Building Greater Humanitarian Capacity

Part Three—Improving U.S. Policy

Part Four—Conclusions

Introduction

Robert I. Rotberg and Thomas G. Weiss

"ONE IMAGE punched through to me," said California Senator Diane Feinstein in explaining why she reversed her original vote in favor of lifting the weapons embargo in Bosnia. "That young woman hanging from a tree. That to me said it all." Senator Feinstein had seen the images on television. "For me, the turning point was the attack on Srebrenica, that weekend with all the missing people."[1]

How well the forces of the media transmit information about overseas crises greatly influences policy-making. Whether directly, by beaming facts and interpretations into the offices of the president of the United States and his principal aides, or indirectly, by affecting the thinking of members of Congress, opinion-makers, or the American public, the way that the media shape and package news from foreign parts is obviously critical. Most Americans learn about the world from television, and most policy-makers from the CNN version of television. The daily press is obviously important, too, for policy- and opinion-makers, but less and less so for the general public. Regional newspapers may report the headlines and the atrocities, but little more.

Whether or not the "CNN factor" is all-powerful (a subject on which the contributors to this book disagree), every chapter in this book and all of the discussions at the original meeting on the subject in late 1994 suggest how important well-informed and well-developed media attention is in the formulation of sensible policies regarding the resolution of

1

ethnic and religious conflict and complex humanitarian crises amid the heightened difficulties of a troubled world at the end of the twentieth century.

In seeking to resolve the imbroglios of Bosnia and prevent future catastrophes like those of Rwanda, nothing is as essential as well-focused, sensitive television and press coverage. Even if Washington understands the real issues, the American public also needs to appreciate those real issues, and the American public depends for its information and inference on the media.

The media have focused international attention on civil wars in Biafra in the late 1960s, in Bangladesh in the early 1970s, and in Ethiopia in 1973 and 1984. In 1994 and 1995, they have shown footage and photos of atrocities in Bosnia and Rwanda; but their attention span is limited, and even the most responsible television directors and newspaper editors can hardly cover every war and all aspects of inhumane attacks on other people. Combat in the Sudan, Liberia, Sierra Leone, Sri Lanka, and Burundi—to mention only a few zones of war—continues, but media attention to these zones is episodic and incomplete.[2]

What can be done by humanitarian agencies to help the media, and how can the media do more—and do more with less?

This book argues that the media's influence on the resolution of post–Cold War crises has taken a quantitative if not qualitative leap forward. The CNN factor is shorthand for this leap forward, but the use of such a term inadequately explains the causal links between information and opinion, on the one hand, and decisions and actions on the other. Despite greater access to information and images—the former head of Médecins Sans Frontières has noted that "the victim and his rescuer have become one of the totems of our age"—neither the public nor policymakers necessarily have a better command of the state of affairs in war zones now than they did a decade ago.[3] Although the connections between the media and political and humanitarian action in civil wars are thus recurrent, the chemistry of the interactions between public exposure and international engagement requires much more serious analytical review than it has received to date.[4]

There is a consensus that technological changes in communications have quickened and sharpened interactions between and among the three key sets of outside actors responding to civil wars: the media, civilian (from both NGOs and the UN) as well as military humanitarian actors, and governmental policy-makers. None of the three sets of institutions is a monolith, however, and analyses that fail to take into account their variegated natures risk obfuscating rather than facilitating understanding.

Although often referred to in the aggregate, the media consist of print and electronic entities, journalists and editors, owners and publishers, and traditional and alternative news organs. Humanitarians comprise nongovernmental, governmental, and intergovernmental groups; presidents and CEOs; headquarters and field staffs; program managers and specialized personnel; and civilian and increasingly militarized versions. Policy-makers include elites as well as mid-level staff in the U.S. State Department, executive branch agencies, and Congress.

All of these institutions have gatekeepers and are hardly immune from considerations of bureaucratic politics and politicking that impede tackling humanitarian agendas effectively. Each media, humanitarian, and governmental organization also has finite financial and human resources, which compels selectivity among options and issues when crises erupt.

Although everyone seems to have a view on these questions—our consumer roles as viewers, listeners, and readers seem to qualify each of us—there are as many anecdotes as there are data. Understanding the interactions among the several actors thus has a special urgency, which is why this book exists. That the media exercised a decisive influence on political decision-makers and on military and humanitarian organizations alike in Somalia and Bosnia and on Congress and President Clinton in Haiti, and that rationales like those of Senator Feinstein are and will constantly be offered, is widely accepted. Yet if the precise role of the media in these crises is to be understood, we need to differentiate between what the media have done and can do and what they do and will not do.

Why, for example, was the December 1992 intervention in Somalia not followed or preceded by an intervention in neighboring southern Sudan, where even more civilians were in danger, or in Angola, where at one point during the civil war 1,000 people were dying per week? Was the lack of TV coverage responsible, or were other political factors more compelling? If policy, as British foreign secretary Douglas Hurd claimed, is not driven by the media, how can one interpret the sudden spiriting away of war-wounded Sarajevans to previously unavailable hospital beds in Britain and beyond?[5] Or again (as the president of United Press International claimed in an effort to delimit the responsibility of the media), why has the war in the Balkans dragged on despite relentless media coverage?[6] Why did we watch the Serbs overrun Srebrenica and Zepa and make a mockery of internationally declared "safe areas"?

The media have quickened the interaction of coverage and policy-making in some instances and in others may have complicated that inter-action unnecessarily. In Somalia, for example, the media played a role in bringing about the military intervention that many (but not all) non-governmental humanitarian agencies had sought. Moreover, the wake of media coverage of the U.S.-led intervention actually brought other oper-ational problems; for instance, more aid workers were killed during the U.S.-led Operation Restore Hope than in the preceding year. The media airing of indignities suffered by dead marines also played a key role in the premature termination of the Western military presence in Somalia.[7] Considering the predictable images—of starvation and war, qat-chewing technicals, live landings on beaches, and the disintegration of the mission—one observer noted that "the military outcome of the operation cannot be easily distinguished from the image of that operation."[8]

The impact of the media on the public's consciousness also proved problematic. As well as dramatizing needs, publicizing human rights abuse, stimulating action, and generating resources, the media have dis-torted the kinds of assistance provided, skewed the allocations of resources and personnel among geographical areas, ignored the role of local humanitarians, and focused international attention on the per-ceived bungling of various agencies. The influence of the media has also posed difficult choices for aid agencies regarding the amount of human and financial resources that they allocate to the cultivation of media relationships rather than to operations. Worst of all, as one journalist has hypothesized, the impact of media coverage may be to "add to the viewer's frustration and cynicism about the ability of his or her govern-ment to do anything about the world's seemingly unsolvable and ever-present problems."[9]

In purveying information, the media help to set the agenda in the foreign policy arena. Here, too, viewpoints differ about the nature of the media as an institution. Some observers see the media as a set of shame-less manipulators that are bound to convey shallow and misinformed conclusions; others view writers and producers as the helpless victims of the harsh economics of their industry.

In disaggregating the media into broadcast (radio and television) and print (newspapers and journals), significant differences appear between news and opinion sources and between those with local or national per-spectives versus those with a global reach. Any analysis must take into account the economic realities that drive a television program or a newspaper to tell a good story ever more quickly and more compellingly than competitors. There are serious tensions contained in the challenges to inform, to entertain, and to persuade.

Part one of this book is entitled "Capitalizing on Technology and Sustaining Media Attention." It first considers the ways in which proliferating information systems and the increasingly commercially driven mass media influence world politics. Does this increased flow represent an opportunity to convey humanitarian messages to a broader public or a threat to confine coverage to more specialized audiences? Second, part one examines the media's coverage of emergencies with a view to exposing measures to increase and sustain attention to emerging and existing crises. How can humanitarian organizations and the media cooperate better to publicize humanitarian issues and ultimately improve policy-making?[10]

Fred Cate's "Communications, Policy-Making, and Humanitarian Crises," analyzes the vital role played by modern communications in circumscribing emergency responses. These include technical systems such as satellites and computers, on-site hardware that permits linkages to persons (both victims and humanitarians) in the theater of conflict, public communications (in particular for the media) that help information flows, and organizational communications that help both humanitarians and policy-makers do their jobs.

Cate asks about the influence of the media (particularly television) on both governmental decision-making and NGO actions, as well as on the rapidly expanding use of advanced information technologies. He argues that new information tools "offer enormous promise but also raise many issues that governments and NGOs have been slow to address." Cate's conclusion is that "media attention, particularly if not sustained, may not be sufficient to generate a response, but it is necessary."

In "Reporting Humanitarianism: Are the New Electronic Media Making a Difference?" Edward R. Girardet—contrary to the prevailing conventional wisdom—is "not convinced that we are in any way better informed today than we were during the 1960s or 1970s."

After examining the positive and negative ways that new technologies are affecting the coverage of humanitarian crises, Girardet argues that both the content and the quality of journalism continue to deteriorate and laments that "the media seem incapable of dealing with more than one issue at a time." He thinks that too many journalists and their gatekeepers have "an obsession with the medium, not with the purpose" of new technologies; he points to the coverage of the Gulf War as "the most shameful episode to date of modern technology journalism." He also finds it unacceptable, particularly in light of the market pressures on editors, that the media constitute "the most powerful institution in the United States without any form of watchdog organization of its own." Appreciating the logistical and informational assistance that international relief agencies provide journalists, Girardet nonetheless cautions his fellow journalists against becoming "overly dependent" on the agencies.

Steven Livingston's chapter, "Suffering in Silence: Media Coverage of War and Famine in the Sudan," combines issues underlying the analyses by Cate and Girardet. He seeks to understand why the appalling suffering of the Sudan's thirty-year-old civil war was and is a "nonstory" in most of the media while its neighbor, Somalia, was so much the focus of media immersion in 1992–93. Livingston asks why the media are "important though fickle players" in their coverage of crises. Along with other authors in this book, he seeks to determine differences in coverage among crises. He insightfully applies "gatekeeping" (from the scholarly literature in communications theory) to "the process by which a nearly infinite array of possible news items is narrowed to the relative handful actually transmitted by the media and heard, read, or seen by audiences."

Livingston's quantitative scrutiny of the *Washington Post*'s coverage of the Sudan and Somalia in the first half of the 1990s is combined with a qualitative interpretation of his interviews with practitioners. He points to several possible partial explanations for the differences in coverage (for example, easier logistics, fewer administrative impediments, and less insecurity). "What is striking is the relative paucity of attention paid to either country," writes Livingston, who explains the dramatic increase in coverage of Somalia as "an extraordinary story, the first totally 'failed' state . . . in modern history." Moreover, after the departure of U.S. troops from Somalia, the news of Rwanda's tragedy took over, lending additional weight to the belief that the media could not cover two humanitarian crises simultaneously. "In each instance, a more intense, concentrated crisis pushed aside any possibility of sustained attention to the Sudan."

Part two of this book, "Building Greater Humanitarian Capacity," examines crisis coverage from the perspective of humanitarian groups and their views about the current limitations of such coverage. It assesses the dangers of the explosion of information without a commensurate increase in the ability of policy-makers to process and understand complex situations. How do humanitarians analyze prospects for responsible journalism? More particularly, how can they help the media maintain high standards when the world's increasingly complex problems are being reduced to sound bites?

Peter Shiras's chapter, "Big Problems, Small Print: A Guide to the Complexity of Humanitarian Emergencies and the Media," examines the reality behind the rhetoric of what are now routinely labeled "complex emergencies"—major crises with many causes that require many responses.

In addition to the dramatic increase in the number and intensity of such emergencies since the end of the cold war, Shiras analyzes the fundamental changes in what political scientists might label the "regime" emerging around recent international responses: the use of the military, the challenges to sovereignty, and the centrality of humanitarian issues to the U.S. foreign policy debate. Shiras analyzes the strengths and weaknesses of the major humanitarian players, both inside and outside of regions of armed conflicts. Most fundamentally, he is troubled by the fact that "both the media and humanitarian organizations are notorious for reducing complex causes to oversimplified and misleading slogans."

John C. Hammock and Joel R. Charny's "Emergency Response as Morality Play: The Media, the Relief Agencies, and the Need for Capacity Building" explores these interactions. The authors introduce into the debate the dilemmas faced by operational NGOs, which are both helped and hindered by the stereotypical images presented of emergencies by the media. The media's "scripted morality play" includes the victims ("teeming masses of suffering Africans or Asians"); the heroes (usually "angels" from the Red Cross and private relief agencies); and the villains ("UN bureaucrats" and "local military authorities"). Most NGOs are happy with this script; it enhances their own visibility and helps their fundraising efforts. Hammock and Charny argue, nevertheless, that it "is ultimately unsatisfying and works against the long-term interests of the relief agencies."

They enumerate what in their experience have been the missing elements from the emergency story that is the media's bill of fare: analyzing root causes of conflict, asking hard questions about the actual credibility of agencies, and emphasizing the ability of local communities to help themselves. Hammock and Charny argue that the scripted morality play can be counterproductive: "The bitter irony in the case of Rwanda, however, is that the relief effort, generally portrayed as a noble success, has had the impact of strengthening the political control over the refugees of the militant Hutu faction responsible for the genocide that created the emergency."

The final chapter in part two is Lionel Rosenblatt's "The Media and the Refugee." His case study explores in depth the interaction between the media and policy-makers from the point of view of a prominent advocacy group seeking to rivet the attention of the easily distracted policy-making community in Washington on the plight of refugees and internally displaced persons. Rosenblatt sees the media as a "natural ally" of public policy advocates. He asks what the difference was between the "faster, more massive, and more successful" responses by the United States to the Kurdish crisis in 1991, the Somali crisis in 1992, the shelling of civilians in Sarajevo in 1993, and the Rwandan genocide in mid-1994 and the U.S. nonresponses to the equally horrific crises in Azerbaijan, the Sudan, Angola, and Liberia. Rosenblatt's answer is straightforward: "prime-time television news coverage," or the "CNN factor."

His thesis, echoing Senator Feinstein, is that "the media have a great deal of short-term influence in creating an instant constituency for appropriate action" but "pay little attention to long-term problems and thus have little interest or influence in preventing or ameliorating humanitarian emergencies." Rosenblatt conceives of emergencies as a special type of narrowly focused event where the media's influence is greatest; hence, he advocates that NGOs "use" the media and argues that, in fact, the media do not mind being so "used." The limitations of the media, in his view, are threefold: they have virtually no interest in covering anticipated events; a problem without media attention cannot really be taken seriously by humanitarians or policy-makers; and the media have a very brief attention span.

Part three, "Improving U.S. Policy," comprises two chapters. The preoccupation in these chapters is the role of the media in the powerful U.S. market and on Washington's decision-makers, although the issues developed in both chapters clearly have much wider implications. The authors discuss the current state of American policy-making with respect to humanitarian crises and the disputed effects of media coverage and public opinion on policy formulation. How do humanitarian concerns fit various definitions of the national interest? Who is the U.S. constituency for humanitarian action in complex emergencies, and what might be done to expand its membership?

In Andrew Natsios's chapter, "Illusions of Influence: The CNN Effect in Complex Emergencies," the author disagrees fundamentally with Rosenblatt. He argues that "the so-called 'CNN effect' has taken on more importance than it deserves as an explanation for responses emanating from the policy-making process in Washington."

Although he recognizes that the media "can influence some policy-makers sometimes," Natsios returns to the starting point of this book, namely that "what has not been carefully studied is when and how that influence occurs." He puts forward three propositions that suggest that the "CNN effect" varies considerably: it is "tangential or irrelevant" when there is a threat to genuine U.S. geopolitical interests; it is "supportive but not central" when a crisis strikes in an area of peripheral geopolitical interest, as long as sufficient resources are available; and it is "a major factor in decision-making" when a peripheral area requires U.S. military force or diplomacy to rally the support of other nations. Natsios concludes his analysis by suggesting that there is a greater payoff from reforms in the humanitarian decision-making apparatus in Washington than there will be from altering purportedly errant media practices.

In "Human Rights and Humanitarian Crises: Policy-Making and the Media," John Shattuck contrasts the Cold War, when human rights threats came largely from "strong governments ruling with an iron hand," with the present era, when abuses result from "weak governments and failed states, and from ethnic and religious conflicts, fanned by cynical political leaders, and made worse by enormous economic, environmental, and demographic pressures." He sees the global movement for human rights as a major new asset for U.S. foreign policy. Carrots can be helpful; but he also views new problems in countries that are in the midst of wrenching changes and civil wars, for which there may be inadequate "sticks."

If "the containment of chaos is the most urgent task facing the international community" and "Rwanda is a new world paradigm," Shattuck argues that increased rather than decreased multilateralism is essential. In attempting to overcome prevailing attitudes in the opposite direction, the media's role is essential even if their character is "morally neutral" and they have shortcomings—"steadily numbing the viewer over time through compassion fatigue" and having "difficulty conveying the history and texture of human rights." The media have the capacity "to educate the public on the new global challenges of human rights and humanitarian crises . . . and to explain why meeting them is in our national interest."

Four central themes dominate this book:

— There is a foreign policy vacuum in the post-post–Cold War era, but the existence of that vacuum signals the opportunity and necessity to reaffirm and reinforce humanitarian principles. The role of the military in humanitarian crises, which is indisputably expanding but with uneven effects, requires clarification.

— Relationships among policy-makers, humanitarian agencies, and the media are complex, even chaotic. But in the current political climate, each needs the other and ought to work better together. Indeed, the pre-vailing political retrenchment in international affairs throughout the West, typified by the priorities of the U.S. 104th Congress, dictates a fresh look by and at each of the three groups. Humanitarian crises should be understood and tackled from all three perspectives in concert, although workable strategies necessitate thinking about each as less than a monolithic entity.

— Public opinion matters, whether to generate the impetus for policy changes, to prepare the public for action, or to ratify policy. The media provide a central nervous system for this constituency-building process.

— New technology in information and mass media has both liberating and constraining implications for the capacity of the international com-munity to respond to complex emergencies. Public education is still the prevailing need on which the new information age should build.

Notes

1. Senator Diane Feinstein, quoted in the *New York Times* (July 28, 1995).

2. For a discussion of several post–Cold War crises, see Larry Minear and Thomas G. Weiss, *Mercy Under Fire: War and the Global Humanitarian Community* (Boulder, Colo., 1995).

3. Rony Brauman, "When Suffering Makes A Good Story," in Médecins Sans Frontières, *Life, Death and Aid* (London, 1993), 154.

4. For an interpretation of the sparse literature, see David Hesmondhalgh, *Media Coverage of Humanitarian Emergencies: A Literature Survey* (London, 1993). See also Jonathan Benthall, *Disasters, Relief and the Media* (London, 1993); and Edward Girardet (ed.), *Somalia, Rwanda and Beyond: The Role of the International Media in Wars and Humanitarian Crises* (Dublin, 1995).

5. See Michael Binyon, "Media's Tunnel Vision Attacked by Hurd," *The Times* (September 10, 1993); Robin Gedye, "Hurd Hits Out Again at Media," *Daily Tele-graph* (September 11, 1993); Michael Leapman, "Do We Let Our Hearts Rule?" *Independent* (September 15, 1993).

6. Louis D. Boccardi, "Luncheon Remarks," Forum on War and Peace in Somalia: The Role of the Media—an International Perspective, Columbia University, February 16, 1994.

7. See Thomas G. Weiss, "Overcoming the Somalia Syndrome—'Operation Restore Hope'?" *Global Governance*, 1 (1995), 171–87.

8. Thomas Keenan, *Back to the Front: Tourisms of War* (Basse-Normandie, 1994), 143.

9. Warren P. Strobel, "TV Images May Shock But Won't Alter Policy," *Christian Science Monitor* (December 14, 1994).

10. For a discussion, see Emily MacFarquhar, Robert I. Rotberg, and Martha A. Chen, *Non-Governmental Organizations, Early Warning, and Preventive Diplomacy* (Cambridge, Mass., 1995).

Part One

CAPITALIZING ON TECHNOLOGY AND SUSTAINING MEDIA ATTENTION

CHAPTER ONE

Communications, Policy-Making, and Humanitarian Crises

Fred H. Cate

NEWS OF THE devastating Los Angeles earthquake reached President Clinton forty minutes after the first shock waves on the morning of January 17, 1994. The president was informed not by officials from the White House, the National Security Council, or even the Federal Emergency Management Agency. Instead, the call came from Housing and Urban Development Secretary Henry Cisneros, who was in the CBS television studios in Washington. After calling his brother in Los Angeles, the president turned for information to the television. "I was able to watch it unfold on television. It was really something."[1]

One year later, the world learned of the devastation in Kobe, Japan, not only through television and other mass media, but through the global network of information networks, the Internet. "The ground was still shaking," John Moran wrote in the *Hartford Courant*, "when university students began firing up their computers to spread word of the disaster."[2] Through electronic mail, messages posted to on-line discussion groups, and the pictures and documents available through the World Wide Web, vital information poured out to government and private relief officials, the news media, worried relatives, and the public at large. In the days that followed the earthquake, although phone service to much of Kobe remained in shambles, the Internet carried requests for supplies, maps, and photographs of the affected area, the names of survivors, and grisly details about the dead and the injured.

The prominent role of the Internet in the aftermath of the Kobe earthquake, like President Clinton's experience after the Northridge earthquake one year earlier, highlights the inextricable link between communications and humanitarian crises. Governments and nongovernmental organizations (NGOs) rely on communications media and technologies to facilitate rapid and widespread responses to humanitarian crises, whenever and wherever they occur. But communications are increasingly called on to play an even broader role in response to complex emergencies.

Humanitarian crises have many causes: natural hazards—earthquakes, floods, winds, landslides, avalanches, cyclones, tsunamis, locust infestations, drought, volcanic eruptions, changes in weather or tidal patterns; human factors—political corruption or malfeasance, warring states or factions, embargoes or blockades, lack of planning or foresight, or simple incompetence; and demographic and geographic characteristics of the affected area—size and density of population, availability of natural resources, and presence or absence of geographic features. Although not all of these causes of humanitarian crises can be prevented or controlled, most can. Therefore, governments and NGOs alike are concerned not only with responding to humanitarian crises, but also with anticipating, mitigating, and resolving them.

Modern communications technologies and media play a vital role in both emergency response and crisis prevention, mitigation, and resolution. Though they often overlap, these roles may be divided into five broad categories:

— *Technical communications systems* (such as satellites, remote sensing devices, and computer networks) and other technology-based communication systems research, predict, track, and provide early warning of approaching crises.

— *On-site communications* maintain links with emergency response officials, the government, affected populations, and sources of emergency relief supplies, transport, and protection.

— *Public communications*—through electronic and print media, wired and cellular telephones, and alternative media—educate the public about complex emergencies; warn of approaching hazards; facilitate participation in public discussions about development, mitigation, and emergency response; and motivate support for political responses.

— *Communication and information for policy formation*, shared among scientists, engineers, government officials, military leaders, other emergency response officials, insurers, the media, and the public, increase knowledge about complex emergencies and how to avoid or resolve them.

— *Organizational communications* are essential for the effective, dependable operation and interaction of private, governmental, and multinational development, mitigation, and relief organizations.

In spite of the widespread recognition of the importance of communication resources in light of humanitarian crises, there has been surprisingly little discussion of the use of communications media and technologies to motivate and facilitate effective policies and priority-setting concerning humanitarian crises, and even less attention paid to the policy (particularly economic and legal) and practical issues raised by these uses of communications resources.

This chapter examines the impact of two significant facets of communication on humanitarian crisis policy-making. The first section addresses the influence of media (particularly television) and direct agency communications with the public on government and NGO policies toward humanitarian crises. This part concludes that direct communications with the public often inadvertently misfocus public attention and therefore, because of the influence of public pressure on policy-makers, run the risk of distorting policy concerning humanitarian crises. The second section examines the rapidly expanding use of advanced information technologies to link agencies and provide the information necessary for rational policy-making. This section concludes that these new information tools, particularly the Internet, offer enormous promise but also raise many issues that governments and NGOs have been slow to address. The failure to resolve the issues raised by both direct communications with the public and new information technologies threatens the capacity of policy-makers to deal effectively with humanitarian crises in the future.

Public Communication

The Power of Mass Media

More than three decades ago Bernard Cohen wrote: "The press may not be successful in telling people what to think, but it is stunningly successful in telling its readers what to think about."[3] Today, that observation would be considered commonplace. Media as a group, and particularly television, have grown to be the most powerful force in American political and social life. Few causes or events, no matter how dramatic they are or how many people are involved, motivate powerful governmental or institutional responses until captured by the cameras of the press.

This result has proven particularly true with international humanitarian crises, where the presence of media attention has played a decisive role in determining political and popular concern about the underlying situation. Michael Beschloss wrote in 1993 that the war in Bosnia was only "the latest example of an overseas crisis in which haunting television pictures arouse the American people to demand their government do something."[4] As the situation in Bosnia illustrates, media attention, particularly if not sustained, may not be sufficient to generate a response, but it is necessary. Before Bosnia, television coverage of the 1991–92 famine in Somalia led to the decision by the United States to launch Operation Restore Hope. The media did not tell government officials anything they did not already know, but their presence made decisive action politically difficult to avoid. The extraordinary film images recorded by Michael Buerk and Mohammed Amin in Wollo and Tigray in 1984, like Jonathan Dimblebey's BBC documentary, "The Unknown Famine," a decade earlier, prompted public and governmental action in Britain. As humanitarian relief workers consistently report, the presence or absence of media attention may mean life or death for affected populations. The media do not change the importance of humanitarian crises, but they significantly affect their impact. "If you can write a nation's stories," George Gerbner once said, "you needn't worry about who makes its laws."[5]

Gerbner's assessment of the power of the media—the nation's storytellers—has not been lost on those who seek to promote action in anticipation of, and response to, humanitarian crises. The role of the public in policy formation is increasingly recognized and exploited by politicians, government agencies, and private organizations wishing to build or undermine support for a proposed humanitarian action. This new recognition, combined with the need of most NGOs to raise money and other resources, has focused attention on ways of informing and motivating the public. In addition, many NGOs have begun to focus on preventing crises or mitigating their impact by educating the public in affected areas about important self-help measures. As a result of all of these and other factors, government and private organizations are increasingly turning to mass media and alternative communications technologies to get their messages out.

The Limits of Mass Media

The power of public communications, however, poses important issues about the capacity of such communications to misinform, distort, and misfocus attention. Accuracy is one of the most important concerns about media reports, particularly when distance and time constraints combine to reduce the opportunity for first-hand evaluation and thorough fact-checking. Consider the earthquake that struck western India in 1993. On September 30, only hours after the worst earthquake in India in fifty years, a *New York Times* headline reported "1,000 Feared Dead."[6] By the following day, the government-controlled Press Trust of India was reporting 6,500 deaths; India state television said 10,000; and local police estimates ran as high as 12,000 fatalities. *USA Today*, however, led with the headline "16,000 feared dead in India."[7] By October 3, the *New York Times* even reported an estimate by one "senior foreign aid official" that as many as 50,000 lives had been lost.[8]

The next day estimates of the death toll were beginning to fall. And by October 6, the *New York Times* reported that the official estimate had been lowered to "fewer than 10,000"—the final death toll—while still offering "unofficial estimates . . . as high as 30,000."[9] This distorted information compromises public confidence and the ability of government and the public to formulate rational, appropriate responses. More importantly, it reflects a broader inattention to accurate, reliable communication, which is essential to saving lives during humanitarian crises.

Even where news reports are accurate, they may distort or mislead, thereby undermining effective policy-making and diminishing public confidence in policymakers and the causes they espouse. In a series of meetings in 1993 examining the effects of media coverage of humanitarian relief efforts, senior officials from the American Red Cross, the BBC, CARE, CNN, the International Broadcasting Trust, the International Federation of Red Cross and Red Crescent Societies (IFRCRCS), U.K. Overseas Development Administration, NPR, Save the Children, and other leading media and relief organizations examined the impact of coverage of humanitarian relief. They recommended practical, specific strategies for both the media and relief organizations to improve the accuracy, timeliness, quality, and cost-effectiveness of the information they disseminate about developing countries. According to the project's final report:

Much of the public throughout the industrialized world shares an image of developing countries that is incomplete and inaccurate. The efforts of the media to alert the public and report the news accurately and promptly, and of relief organizations to motivate public and governmental support and save human lives, inadvertently contribute to this image. Because western audiences often lack knowledge of developing countries, reports of exceptional events, such as famines or floods, may foster misimpressions of the developing world.[10]

Surveys suggest that these impressions are widespread and dramatic. For example, a 1993 World Vision UK public opinion survey concluded that the "public has a grossly distorted view of the Third World."[11] Fewer than half of all respondents knew that loan repayments from developing countries exceed the aid they receive from more developed countries.

Causes of these misimpressions are not difficult to identify. Most news media report the extraordinary, not the ordinary. As Peter Adamson, author of the annual *Progress of Nations* and *State of the World's Children* reports, has noted:

From our own everyday experience we know that what appears on the news—the crimes, the deaths, the rapes, the motorway accidents, etc.—do not represent the norms of our societies; we know they are exceptions to daily life. That is what makes them news. When we take them on board, we do so against the ballast of our own everyday experience and knowledge of life in our own societies.

But when it comes to the developing world, most of the public have no personal experience; they have not been to the developing world. They have no ballast—no equivalent sense of the norms, the unexceptional aspects of life in the developing world—to set against the constant reporting of the exceptional.[12]

Most media report on "news" events, not issues or slow-developing processes. Particularly with increased reliance on television news sources, the dramatic story with compelling video about a specific event is the mainstay of Western news. Many times the links between important information and stories that appear "newsworthy" in the eyes of the media and the public are difficult to establish, as suggested by a recent Food and Agriculture Organization (FAO) report. "When images of tortured starving faces and the bloated bellies of dying children lead the nightly news, the world rushes food and assistance to the hungry. As the food aid arrives, it feeds the news as well as the starving."[13] Despite the impression of many Western observers that Africa is "a continent of recurring famine," the FAO report continued, it is drought, not famine, that is Africa's "principal natural disaster. . . . Famine is not the necessary outcome of drought. There are proven strategies to reduce the effects of drought and prevent even the most vulnerable populations from starving." In 1992, for example, twelve southern African countries were hit by a drought that caused greater crop failure than Ethiopia, the Sahel, and the Horn of Africa faced in 1984–85. But a rapid response by the countries involved, as well as international organizations such as the FAO, prevented that drought from causing famine. "The unprecedented early response prevented a famine and as such a major news story." What went largely unreported, the FAO concluded, was the "story about millions who could have died but did not."

Broadcast news, in particular, is often composed largely of negative stories, in part, because the public prefers these and, also, because negative news represents exceptional events. This is especially true of news about developing countries. The Third World and Environment Broadcasting Project reported in 1993 that two-thirds of mainstream international news coverage about developing countries concentrated on conflicts and disasters. The focus on tragedy has a demonstrable impact on policy-makers and on the public. In his opening address to the 1994 World Conference on Natural Disaster Reduction, Olavi Elo, secretary-general of the International Decade for Natural Disaster Reduction (IDNDR) Secretariat, stressed:

> Societies are so overwhelmed by human emergencies, by human disasters, that we have halted in our tracks, as it were, on the road to progress and development, to stand helplessly by, paralyzed, watching so many human tragedies unravel before our eyes. We are not helped by how the priorities are perceived in the eyes of the media: human misery is far more newsworthy than a population that has been made safe and sound. In short, an earthquake or flood that does little or no damage is not news.[14]

Event-based coverage is often limited both by the time of each report (often 60 or 90 seconds) and by the time that media will stay with a developing story (rarely longer than a few weeks). The media's interest, like the public's, is often short-lived. This type of coverage does not lend itself to covering complex, complicated subjects, whether development or a banking scandal. The issues of crisis prevention and mitigation, particularly when intertwined with development, are enormously complex and difficult to convey in brief news reports. Consider just one example—famine. Although not a primary feature of the developing world, famine is one of the topics from the developing world most widely reported by Western media. Yet the causes of famine are numerous and complex and often develop over long periods of time. While news reports tend to focus on drought—certainly an important cause of famine—other significant causes include war, tribal conflict, civil unrest, poverty, unemployment, livestock loss, corruption, and government inefficiency. Famines are usually long-term processes, not events. Consider the findings in the IFRCRCS's *World Disaster Report 1993*, concerning the famine that peaked in Sudan in 1985:

> While two decades of declining rainfall were the most obvious and immediate cause of the food shortages, famine was the product of a complex process that increased the vulnerability of many Sudanese until the disaster took place.
>
> That process included the government's low and late investment in peasant rain-fed agriculture and livestock production, poor infrastructure and limited formal credit. . . .
>
> The government also failed to maintain adequate food reserves, choosing to allow exports instead, under pressure from Sudanese farmers and merchants, and from international banks wanting loan repayments.[15]

Many media are understandably ill equipped to deal with the often complex and ill-focused issues surrounding humanitarian crises.

Alternatives to Mass Media

Given the inherent limitations of most media and the different objectives of NGOs and the news media, many organizations are beginning to recognize that coverage by established news media is not the only means for communicating with the public. Many humanitarian agencies have noted the opportunities to create and air their own programming on cable television, public broadcasting stations, and satellite television, and to explore alternative formats to news coverage, such as educational or even entertainment programming. The One World Group of Broadcasters has worked with producers in developing countries to create its *Developing Stories* series, which has been distributed in eighteen countries throughout the developed world. The U.S. Corporation for Public Broadcasting has also begun exploring ways of working with "public" broadcasters in other countries to share production costs in joint ventures to create new markets for existing programming. The Federal Emergency Management Agency (FEMA) and the American Red Cross have worked together to develop *Disaster Dudes*, a television show for children that provides educational messages about disaster preparedness. During the 1994 Los Angeles earthquake, FEMA distributed information directly to the public as an insert called *Disaster Times* in *USA Today*.

Many humanitarian relief and development organizations are attempting to reach the public, as well as each other, through information networks available via the Internet. For example, more than a dozen NGOs have joined ReliefNet, an electronic forum through which these organizations provide information and solicit contributions. ReliefNet, in turn, is linked to other database networks, such as PeaceNet, ConflictNet, EcoNet, and EnviroWeb, which promote interest in more focused humanitarian and environmental causes.

Direct agency communications with the public, however, also pose serious issues. In addition to concerns related to financial resources and expertise required for effective communications, agency-sponsored communications may distort public perceptions. Many relief organizations compete against each other and against other issues and institutions for public support. To attract and maintain that support, organizations seek to draw attention to themselves and to the needs of the developing world. Like the media, these organizations therefore have a considerable incentive to stress negative news about developing countries; to focus on single, dramatic events, like disasters; to suggest simplistic solutions (for example, giving money); and to exaggerate the role of Western aid and minimize the importance of indigenous relief efforts.

Consider this report from Peter Adamson, speaking to a meeting of UNICEF's National Committees:

> Some of you may have seen the recent series of advertisements for the Save the Children Fund. These advertisements state, in a headline, that "13,000 children die every day from dehydration—your 20 cents can save this life."

If that were true, then all 13,000 of those daily deaths could be prevented for 13,000 times 20 cents—about $2,500—far less than the cost of this meeting. The annual cost of preventing all dehydration deaths—a third of all child deaths in the world each year—would be about one million dollars, far less than the cost of the *State of the World's Children* report.

What are we saying to the public? They too can do these sums. And eventually, I am sure, cynicism will set in and we will simply not be believed—nor will we deserve to be. For, with the best intentions in the world, we are not telling the truth.[16]

Moreover, although NGOs frequently have considerable resources in developing countries and may have experience with their cultures and languages, these organizations are often unable to draw strategically on those resources to correct Western misperceptions. This inability is due in part to the financial instability of many relief organizations, which makes strategic, long-term planning difficult. Also, even the largest international relief organizations find themselves overwhelmed by the need to respond to emergencies. Planning and executing thoughtful strategies for better informing the media and the public appear to be far lower priorities. In addition, many organizations seek to do everything themselves—administer their organizations, raise money, collect and distribute relief supplies, inform the media and the public, and perform many other disparate tasks. In short, by attempting to do too much, these organizations often lack the resources and the expertise to do all of these tasks effectively. Effective, thoughtful public communications often fall by the wayside.

These issues are increasingly being recognized and addressed by leading relief and mitigation organizations. For example, InterAction—a membership association of U.S. relief organizations and a leader in addressing communications issues—requires its members to "respect the dignity, values, history, religion, and culture of the people served by the programs. They shall neither minimize nor overstate the human and material needs of those whom it assists."[17] In January 1995, InterAction hosted a meeting of leading U.S. humanitarian relief organizations to consider whether these standards should be strengthened. Save the Children (UK) has also adopted standards for communicating with the public: "The images and text used in all communications must be accurate and should avoid stereotypes and cliches. . . . Attempts should be made where possible to identify and quote people being photographed or interviewed. If they wish to remain anonymous, their request should be honored. Wherever possible, the views and experiences of the people involved should be communicated."[18]

Recommendations

Meetings such as the Roundtable on the Media, Scientific Information, and Disaster Relief at the World Conference in Yokohama, and those leading up to publication of *Media, Disaster Relief and Images of the Developing World,* have resulted in a variety of specific recommendations to help address the issues faced by both media and humanitarian relief organizations. Although few are new, they are instructive and noteworthy for the collaborative processes from which they emerged. They include the following recommendations:

Strategies for the Media

Use news resources more effectively. The media face the challenge to identify resources that could provide early notification about developing stories; background information; and timely, accurate reports about events in developing countries. Independent journalists or "stringers" could be used more widely. More cooperative ventures among news organizations could make maintaining bureaus in developing countries more economically feasible.

Work with relief organizations where possible. Relief organizations often have the infrastructure within developing countries to help the media identify important issues or emerging trends, give logistical support in reporting those stories, provide background information, and arrange for sources and spokespeople from within the relevant country or countries.

Designate and train development journalists. Reporting on developing countries could be improved by increasing the number of reporters who cover the area and by designating "development correspondents." Media organizations should consider how reporters and photographers who are rushed into a country to cover a story can be better prepared for such assignments, how they can have the greatest amount of time possible "on the scene," how that time can best be used, and what training or information would help editors and other gatekeepers within the media evaluate the significance of stories from developing countries and place those stories in a broader news context.

Cover efforts by indigenous organizations and individuals to mitigate crises. Reporting should seek to include, to an extent proportional to their importance, relief efforts by indigenous people and organizations or by other developing countries. The media should seek to interview and quote officials from indigenous governments and relief organizations where possible, and to report specific measures that have either succeeded or failed to reduce the impact of humanitarian crises.

Provide professional training and review. Journalism reviews, graduate schools, professional societies, and media critics should play an important role in training journalists in international reporting, critiquing reporting on developing countries, and sensitizing both the media and the public. There are noteworthy examples of high-quality reporting on development issues; these should be noted, rewarded, and used to help train other reporters, editors, photographers, and producers.

Expand self-analysis and review. Media organizations are encouraged to evaluate their reporting about humanitarian crises and, where appropriate, to work with relief organizations to improve the quality, accuracy, and thoroughness of such reporting. The media should also be aware of, and sensitive to, competitive pressures or inadequate resources that might compromise accuracy or thoroughness in reporting.

Strategies for Agencies

Articulate communications strategy. Each relief organization should publicly articulate its strategy for communicating with the media and the public and clarify the purposes of those communications. Communications strategies, like all activities of relief organizations, should be evaluated regularly to determine their effectiveness, relationship to the organization's goals, and impact. Relief organizations should also regularly evaluate their communications strategies for their impact on public understanding and ethical and professional appropriateness.

Expand relationships. Governments and NGOs should seek to develop working relationships with the media based on mutual trust and the recognition of differing characteristics, goals, and needs. Regular, effective communication among these disparate groups before, during, and after disaster "events" can greatly enhance those relationships.

Train organization personnel to work with media. Relief organizations should provide training (particularly for personnel in the field) on how to work with media to improve the timeliness, quality, and accuracy of reporting about developing countries. Relief organizations are often well placed to help the media identify and report important stories accurately and sensitively, evaluate the quality of news reports, and correct inaccurate stories or supplement incomplete ones. For example, field offices could help identify stories warranting press coverage and provide indigenous spokespeople, logistical support, and other assistance to media covering stories in developing countries.

Provide reliable, useful information. Governments and NGOs should seek to provide reliable information to the media, as early as possible, in a concise and readily understandable form. Relief organizations should recognize that the media have limited resources and should avoid overstating the scope of humanitarian crises.

Identify themes and trends. Governments and NGOs should seek to identify and communicate specific themes and messages, both through the mass media and through other alternative forms of communication. Organizations should help link important stories to newsworthy events that are traditionally covered by Western media, such as meetings of the World Bank or the International Monetary Fund.

Evaluate media content. Relief organizations should evaluate media coverage for accuracy, quality, completeness, timeliness, and professionalism. Excellent media coverage should be recognized and used to help improve other reporting. Inaccuracies or misperceptions should be corrected through direct contact with the media and reporters involved, letters to the editor, guest columns, counterinformation, and other means available to relief organizations.

Create alternative programming. Relief organizations should work to facilitate documentaries and other programming that provide a more complete image of developing countries. In particular, organizations should work cooperatively with program producers in developing countries and with the media to create and disseminate programming. New outlets such as cable and satellite television offer considerable potential for airing such programming.

Evaluate relief organization communications. Many relief organizations—individually and cooperatively—have adopted standards for their communications with the public. All communications activities should be evaluated according to articulated standards.

Organizational Communications and Information Resources

Both humanitarian relief agencies and governmental organizations have long relied on effective communications to organize their individual and collective actions and to collect and provide the information necessary for effective policy-making. Humanitarian organizations, like virtually all business, governmental, and academic institutions, have benefited significantly from the widespread improvement in telecommunications infrastructures and digital equipment. Many of these organizations, however, because of their far-flung activities, need for rapid response, and often limited resources have been particularly aided by the increased reliability and versatility and decreased size and cost of many of these technologies. A 1992 report on the communications and information resources of the IFRCRCS noted the unusual demands of the IFRCRCS, with its more than 150 national societies, and the dramatic capacity of communications technologies and improved information management simultaneously to "enhance the Federation's individual and collective ability to make more timely and informed decisions and reinforce its position in disaster preparedness, relief and rehabilitation."[19]

The most dramatic use of communications technologies within the humanitarian relief community has been in the area of information networks. These networks range from local area networks, linking computers, printers and other peripherals, and telecommunications modems within a single office or among the geographically far-flung offices of a single organization, to advanced, interactive, searchable databases interconnected via direct links, dial-up access, or the Internet.[20] The Internet's many types of services may generally be divided into three categories:

electronic mail messages (e-mail), through which one user can communicate privately with another or with a service provider; electronic bulletin boards, where users can post messages for all other bulletin board subscribers to read and can read and respond to the messages posted by all other users;[21] and on-line services, products, and databases, such as electronic catalogs from which a user can order merchandise, make on-line airline reservations, and search more than 2,200 databases. Some on-line services offer only text while others provide graphics, photographs, video, and sound as well as text.

All three categories of Internet services offer enormous promise for organizations concerned with humanitarian crises. Many of these groups already take advantage of e-mail. The IFRCRCS, for example, has begun using Internet e-mail to communicate with its more than 150 national societies. The two most recent (and potentially most powerful) uses of the Internet by the humanitarian relief community are for collecting urgent, real-time information about humanitarian crises from the affected areas and for linking remote information resources about complex emergencies.

The Internet as a Medium for Rapid, Emergency Communications

The response to the Northridge and Kobe earthquakes clearly demonstrated the power and resilience of electronic information networks, joined together through the Internet, to link areas affected by humanitarian crises with the outside world. Electronic messages about the Northridge quake were reported on the Internet within twenty minutes of the first shocks. One commercial on-line provider, Prodigy, established a free bulletin board called "LA Earthquake"; 500 messages were posted during the first few hours. The Internet's role in Japan was even more dramatic. Students at Kobe City University of Foreign Studies reported that "the Network is still alive and in the normal condition," and news of the quake soon dominated bulletin boards, discussion groups, and private e-mail. Other Japanese universities and companies with Internet connections, such as NTT and Sony, soon began carrying reports or sharing their computing capacity to help bear the load. These sites were, in turn, "mirrored" by sites in the United States and elsewhere, which carried copies of the information in an effort to reduce pressure on strained Japanese facilities. A special Internet chat channel, called "Kobe," was established for people to share real-time data about the quake.

The information available included daily and even hourly reports by

Kobe residents, foreign visitors, and emergency personnel. Relief organizations in Japan and around the world shared information, including
maps of the city, aerial photographs of the damage, lists of supplies
needed, offers of aid and volunteers, news about survivors, and lists of
the dead and injured. The messages got through, even though much of
Kobe lost telephone service, and telephone lines into other parts of Japan
were clogged, because the Internet was originally created by the U.S.
Department of Defense to withstand a nuclear attack. Messages automatically route around downed lines or broken connections and can be
transmitted through and backed up on remote sites. Despite fears that
advanced digital technologies might not withstand severe natural
hazards, the Internet proved its usefulness in linking crisis-affected areas
with the rest of the world and in coordinating emergency relief efforts.

These technologies have demonstrated their effectiveness in response
to natural catastrophes. Their applicability to fast-moving, complex
emergencies like those in Rwanda in April and May 1994 is clear.

Internet Databases

Humanitarian relief agencies are also increasingly relying on the
Internet to organize, share, and analyze information, whether about specific complex emergencies, collaborative activities, or other issues of
interest. Three examples may help identify both the enormous potential
and the significant issues raised by these innovations.

One of the earliest databases on humanitarian crises was created by the
Centre for Research on the Epidemiology of Disasters (CRED), located at
the Université Catholique de Louvain. Funded by the General Administration for Cooperation and Development of the Government of Belgium,
CRED works closely with the World Health Organization, the World
Meteorological Organization, the United Nations Department for Humanitarian Affairs (DHA), IFRCRCS, and the Agency for International Development's Office of Foreign Disaster Assistance (AID/OFDA). CRED
maintains the Emergency Disaster Events Database (EM-DAT), which
contains data on more than 9,000 disasters from 1900 to the present (most
since 1960). This information is available to governments, disaster mitigation organizations, and academics for vulnerability assessment, policy
formation, and research. EM-DAT data include onset date; type of disaster; country; continent; affected population; estimated economic damage;
and number of dead, injured, and homeless.

Although accurate, comparable data are often difficult to obtain and verify, they are collected from the U.S. AID/OFDA (33 percent); major insurance companies such as Royale Belge, Munich-Re, and Swiss-Re (18 percent); UN DHA (16 percent); and other multinational, government, and private organizations. CRED regularly publishes summary data from the EM-DAT; in addition, the database is accessible at CRED's Brussels office and through other on-line disaster information databases, as discussed below.

The second example of information databases is the server provided by FEMA.[22] Available on the Internet in both graphic (through World Wide Web) and text (through Gopher and Telnet) formats, FEMA's database provides overview about the agency and its mission and access to a series of files ranging from "Disaster Assistance" to "Volcanoes" through either a library structure or a master index. This server, parts of which are still under construction, is one of a rapidly growing number that serve three separate functions. It introduces the user to the agency and thus provides an important public relations function. The server provides practical information about what the agency's services are, how to use them, and how to contact the agency. Finally, it provides access to a database of substantive information about humanitarian crises, particularly natural disasters.

Similar services are provided by most U.S. federal government agencies, including AID/OFDA; many state agencies, such as the State of California's Governor's Office of Emergency Services; the United Nations; the Asian Disaster Preparedness Center; InterAction; and the Alliance for a Global Community.[23]

The third and most powerful type of electronic information service uses the capabilities of the Internet to combine a wide range of decentralized data resources across the humanitarian relief community. This most advanced type of electronic information system capitalizes on the Internet's capacity to carry large amounts of information (including text, image, and sound files) and to link distant data resources (for example, a database on natural hazards in one country with a collection of digital maps in another).

One of the earliest prototype systems designed to harness the power of the Internet in anticipation of humanitarian crises was the Emergency Preparedness and Information Exchange (EPIX).[24] Originally based on a series of text menus and available via Gopher, an early information search and retrieval mechanism, EPIX is now available through the

World Wide Web, although it is still limited to text files. A later, similar system, the Disaster Reduction Information Exchange (DRIX), provided access to information on disaster prevention, mitigation, and preparedness. Information provided through DRIX was "intended to assist in policy formulation and planning, statistics gathering, research and awareness-raising that can be used to increase knowledge about and strengthen capacities for disaster prevention, mitigation and preparedness."[25] DRIX contained links to servers maintained by many government and private organizations, such as those listed previously.

Whereas the focus of DRIX was on disaster preparedness, the Facility for International Readiness and Response to Emergencies (FIRRE) provides access to information for use in "monitoring, early warning, and alert of possible, incipient or ongoing emergencies and natural disasters, and for the purpose of preparing, facilitating, conducting and coordinating effective and timely international response."[26] Although still under construction, FIRRE presently contains computer links to databases about "Current Emergency Situations" (including situation reports compiled by Volunteers in Technical Assistance), "Humanitarian Assistance" (including a wide range of information about refugees, human rights, emergency relief statistics and supplies, and relief organizations), "Daily News Bulletins and Current Affairs," "Country-Specific Information" (including country profiles from the U.S. State Department and the CIA World Factbook, and maps from the World Map Collection at the University of Texas and the Canadian National Atlas Information Service), "Natural Hazards" (including current weather maps and satellite images), and "Monitoring Programmes" (such as the World Food Program Food Aid Monitor).

In 1994, a number of multinational, governmental, private, and academic organizations and specialists joined to create a prototype system combining the capabilities of EPIX, DRIX, and FIRRE. The International Emergency Reduction, Readiness/Response Information System (IERRIS) prototype used advanced telecommunications and computer technologies to provide both a single entry point to the databases of public and private humanitarian relief agencies throughout the world and a data structure that combined field reporting, warnings, and relief status reporting into a coherent whole. As stated in the IERRIS Project Abstract:

> The Project is to enable the actors concerned to: adopt information management procedures that are of common benefit; work with

common and/or compatible information management standards and technologies; collaborate in the development of new information systems and procedures so as to meet information needs that are not met by existing systems and procedures and share and exchange suitable emergency-related information collected for respective institutional needs. This concerted effort will result in major improvements in the quality, specificity and timeliness of information available internationally for early warning monitoring reporting, resource mobilization, and coordination, evaluation, disaster reduction, and the information exchange, reference and referral services related to all these concerns.[27]

The IERRIS prototype,[28] based at the Centre for Policy Research on Science and Technology at Simon Fraser University, provided a powerful, easy to use graphic interface that linked data (including text, hypertext, pictures, video, and audio) relevant to disaster preparedness, monitoring, and response. The prototype expanded the availability of data that are available on-line through government and private databases, making data more convenient and less costly to access and providing them in a format most useful for further distribution or analysis. These benefits, in turn, create an incentive for more organizations to make their information related to humanitarian crises available on-line. The IERRIS prototype has clearly shown the value of such a system and has provided important information to emergency management professionals designing future interoperable systems. Having demonstrated its effectiveness, the IERRIS prototype was essentially terminated at the end of 1994.

A consortium of international, governmental, private, and academic organizations is constructing an operational system called HazardNet, building on the IERRIS experience. Based at the Centre for Policy Research on Science and Technology at Simon Fraser University, HazardNet's goal "is to enhance the timeliness, quality, quantity, specificity and accessibility of information for persons and organizations worldwide concerned with preventing, mitigating, preparing for or responding to large-scale natural and technological emergencies."[29]

Although still under development, HazardNet offers four services: (1) access to historical and scientific information about natural hazards through an easy-to-use, icon-based interface; (2) access to real-time hazard alerts, warnings and forecasts, situation reports, and news accounts; (3) a map display identifying the locations of hazardous events and through which users will be able to acquire the latest information about a specific hazard or emergency and any ongoing response activities; and (4) a system through which governmental agencies and NGOs can share information and communicate effectively with each other.

Like IERRIS, HazardNet does not provide information on humanitarian crises unrelated to natural hazards or technological accidents. The system, however, demonstrates the power of electronic information resources to integrate and facilitate the resources and activities of diverse humanitarian response agencies. It also demonstrates ways in which future collaborative systems might provide graphic, textual, video, and audio information on all forms of humanitarian crises.

Issues Posed by Information Technologies

Uses of information technologies, particularly the Internet, raise a number of significant issues, some of which are specifically related to the technologies involved. For example, electronic information has thus far proven difficult to authenticate and therefore often raises questions about provenance and integrity. These issues are presented in many different contexts. For example, one organization may provide accurate data, in an e-mail message or in a database, that are subsequently altered. The alteration may be deliberate (for example, by an agency or government wishing to exaggerate the extent of need or the quality of response being provided, or by an unauthorized user) or accidental (for example, a typographical error or mislabeling of data). In either case, subsequent users will be hard pressed to identify alterations because digital information is extraordinarily malleable. Unlike printed or analog information, it is easily and undetectably altered.

The quality of electronic information may also be at issue because it is often difficult to identify the source of the data reliably or because the source may be unrecognizable. With most Internet services, it is easy to post data on an electronic server or bulletin board without the "filters" of peer review or statistical analysis or the credibility of recognized institutions or publications. In fact, every Internet user is also a potential data supplier; consider, for example, the students at Kyoto City University of Foreign Studies whose reports about the Kyoto earthquake appeared alongside reports from the IFRCRCS and United Nations. The variations among the different lists of people killed by that earthquake raise similar issues: where were those lists from, how were they compiled, and who vouched for their accuracy? Despite the best intentions of all the people involved, inaccurate, imprecise, or misidentified data may be posted.

The accuracy of information provided on the Internet may also be compromised because of how data are replicated and accessed. Many Internet databases, such as HazardNet, do not actually maintain all of the information they reference. Instead, they provide electronic links to other data sets. This is a valuable attribute of these resources. But these linkages also create potential concerns about the authenticity and accuracy of data, which the database provider references but does not originate or control. Thus, although these providers may be clearly identified and highly reputable, they cannot necessarily be held responsible for the accuracy of the data. This same powerful capacity of the Internet to support an unlimited number of links to the same data set also increases the likelihood that inaccurate or incomplete data will be made widely available or used for purposes for which it was never intended.

To date, Internet data providers deal with these issues by labeling their on-line resources "experimental." Other, more lasting solutions are being tested, however. One of these provides electronic data "signatures" that could not be separated from a specific data file and would indicate where that file was originated and whether it had been altered. Limiting access to authorized users only is another effective tool. However, any measure for guaranteeing data integrity that restricts access also limits the usefulness of the information resource and may increase its cost. In short, it has thus far proven difficult to guarantee the origin, authenticity, or accuracy of networked information without also compromising the very features that make such information so valuable.

To be valuable, information must be not only accurate, but also dependable. Thus far, electronic platforms, such as individual servers and the telephone or backbone links that connect them, have demonstrated uneven reliability. In the event of disaster or political or civil unrest, the technologies and the institutions that keep the Internet or other networks functioning are likely to be at risk. As many Internet users have found, to their annoyance, heavy rains or high winds will often cause the network or some key component to "crash." Yet the experience following the Northridge and Kobe earthquakes suggests that these systems may be more reliable than many observers had anticipated.

Even when complete failure is avoided, however, networks and servers face real limits in terms of speed and capacity. After the Northridge and Kobe quakes, some users found important messages delayed or rejected because of high system use; some servers were unavailable during periods of peak demand. Growing at a rate of approximately 141 percent per year, key transmission routes and services on the Internet already are overloaded, contributing to system brownouts. For example, e-mail users in the United States, generating more than 100 million messages every day, are discovering that when electronic mailboxes are full (a function of technology and system operator preferences), excess e-mail is rejected, often without notification to either the sender or the recipient.

The key issue is not the current reliability of the Internet, but the need for certainty as to its future reliability. Dramatically escalating use, increased privatization, and the fact that many key Internet links and resources are maintained by universities and companies with limited resources to guarantee system reliability, threaten the future stability of the Internet and warrant careful scrutiny.

Problems of accuracy, reliability, and capacity are serious but are likely to be managed, if not solved, with technology. Other issues—such as how to pay the cost of these services and guarantee access to them—may not be dealt with so easily. The Internet is financed today through a combination of government and other public institutional support, connection charges, advertising, and direct subscriptions. There is little uniformity among users and among countries as to how much is paid or by whom.

Under the current system, an outgrowth of Internet's origins as a government-funded network, few users pay the actual costs of their use, and no users pay distance-sensitive costs. If one user in New York sends an e-mail to another user in Geneva, the sender may pay an access charge or subscription fee, but she is unlikely to pay her own "infrastructure" costs—they are most likely to be borne by an institutional intermediary, such as a university or employer—and she is certain not to pay the actual transmission cost (for example, the cost of a phone call from New York to Geneva). This may help explain the attractiveness to the users of the Internet as a communications medium.

As the Clinton administration, the 104th Congress, and other governments move to privatize the Internet and eliminate government subsidies, more costs will almost certainly be passed on to users. An intercontinental e-mail message is unlikely to be free to the user, or billed only as a subscription fee or connection charge. Instead, like virtually all other telecommunications traffic, it will be billed at actual cost, based on the distance, data volume, or time involved. In the past year, commercial services have come to dominate the Internet. The move toward privatization and commercialization is accelerating, and with it will come increased pressure on information services to cover their costs. Most of the existing disaster-related databases rely on university and government resources for their computing and storage capacity and Internet connections. These institutions are able to provide them, in part, because of their low cost. As those costs increase—and they are certain to do so—many government agencies and NGOs are likely to feel the squeeze.

Closely related to the issue of cost is that of access, particularly in the area affected by the humanitarian crisis itself. Regulations often create barriers to access, usually in one of two ways. First, national customs regulations often restrict the transborder movement of advanced technologies, either because the exporting country wishes to control their dissemination or because the importing country seeks to restrict the flow of information that many of these technologies facilitate.[30] Second, national broadcasting regulations and frequency assignments can limit or delay the use of communications technologies that "compete" with national telecommunications service providers or require radio spectrum assigned for other uses.

Hans Zimmerman, of DHA, has described the "sad experience of those who provide international humanitarian assistance in the age of information superhighways":

If anywhere on the ocean a vessel with a crew of one is in distress, all related communications have absolute priority and are free of charge. This is stipulated in some 50 international regulatory instruments, from Article 1 of the Constitution of the International Telecommunication Union all the way to number 2923, Article 37 in Chapter IX of the Radio Regulations. The necessity for absolute priority of Distress signals has been recognized worldwide, ever since the 14th of April 1912, when the *Titanic* hit an iceberg.

If after an earthquake some 10,000 persons are trapped under the debris of their houses, any customs official can prevent the arriving rescue teams from importing their walkie-talkies. And any official can prevent the teams in [the country] from using their communications equipment, unless they first obtain a license from a national telecommunications authority, whose building might just have collapsed in the earthquake. And if a team is, by chance, nevertheless able to use its satellite terminal, they are three months later presented with telephone bills for tens of thousands of dollars.[31]

These and other regulatory limits on access have been the subject of ongoing international discussions and reports, including the 1990 International Conference on Disaster Communications in Geneva and the 1991 Conference on Disaster Communications in Tampere, Finland. The latter meeting resulted in *The Tampere Declaration on Disaster Communications*, calling upon nations to, among other things, "minimize regulatory barriers, such as customs clearance procedures and data protection laws, to rapid dissemination of information and effective use of communication resources essential for disaster management."

The International Telecommunication Union (ITU) plenipotentiary, meeting in Kyoto in September 1994, finally acted on the *Tampere Declaration* by passing Resolution COM 4/14, creating an Inter-Agency Working Group on Emergency Telecommunications in preparation for an intergovernmental conference on emergency telecommunications in 1996. Although progress has been slow, its pace appears to be increasing.

Regulatory provisions are not the only restrictions on access to information technologies. Important questions remain to be answered: Will disaster information services be available to all organizations, in more and less developed countries, who desire access? Will they be available in the field and in countries without data-quality switched networks? Will they be available to organizations without network access or technological expertise? Will they, because of their power and flexibility, begin to replace information resources such as printed material?

These questions, while important, are not intended to detract from the promise that information technologies hold for preventing and ameliorating humanitarian crises. In many ways, precisely because of their versatility and lower cost, electronic information resources have the potential for dramatically expanding access. But the very real threat of escalating costs, regulatory obstacles, and the infrastructure and skill requirements to use these resources should at least be the subject of full discussion.

Information networks and databases must comply not only with the laws of the jurisdiction in which they are located, but also with the laws of the jurisdiction in which they are received. For information resources available via the Internet, that involves more than 100 separate national legal regimes, not to mention state or territorial laws. For example, in one instance, electronic image files, which were located in California and which contained photographs that were almost certainly not considered obscene in that state, were downloaded in Tennessee, where they were found to be obscene. As a result, the California operator was held liable under Tennessee law.

This is serious business for many national governments, concerned about the economic or cultural effects of unbridled information flows. As Anne Branscomb, author of *Who Owns Information?*, has written: "The very existence of information technology is threatening to nation states."[32] Although obscenity laws are unlikely to be pose a problem for most NGOs, laws governing privacy and intellectual property may create greater risks.

Under the European Union's *Council Directive on the Protection of Individuals With Regard to the Processing of Personal Data and on the Free Movement of Such Data*, member states will be required to enact laws protecting personal privacy and prohibiting the transmission of personal information to countries such as the United States, which are perceived as ignoring privacy concerns. Under the directive, every member state would have to enact laws ensuring, among other things, that personal data—defined broadly by the directive as "any information relating to an identified or identifiable natural person"[33]—must be accurate, relevant, not excessive, and used only for the legitimate purposes for which it was collected. Personal data may be collected, processed, or transmitted only with the consent of the data subject. The collection and processing of data revealing "racial or ethnic origin, political opinions, religious beliefs, philosophical or ethical persuasion . . . [or] concerning health or sexual life" are severely restricted. The data subject must be informed and provided with certain mandatory disclosures if data are to be collected, processed, and/or distributed to a third party. In addition, he or she must have access to the data and must have the opportunity to object to the data's collection and processing and/or disclosure. He or she must also have the opportunity to correct any factual errors.

How many relief workers could comply with these requirements in the field? How many organizations can guarantee that the information they post to the Internet meets these stringent requirements? Yet, if the data are moved into or out of Europe, this is the law that will apply. Already, the British Data Protection Registrar, acting under national law, forbade a proposed sale of a British mailing list to a United States direct mail organization. The French *Commission Nationale de L'informatique et des Libertés* has required that identifying information be removed from patient records before they were transferred to Belgium, Switzerland, and the United States. Europe represents only one group of countries whose laws will be applicable to data on the Internet; there is a diversity of other national regulatory structures in place for protecting personal privacy.

Even data that do not leave the United States are likely to be the subject of privacy-related regulation, particularly if the federal government is involved in its collection or storage. Concern about privacy is growing. According to the 1992 Equifax survey by Louis Harris & Associates and Alan Westin, 76 percent of Americans report feeling that they have lost control over personal information about themselves, and 79 percent are concerned about threats to personal privacy.[34] The proliferation of digital technologies has sparked growing concern over personal privacy and heightened interest in data protection and privacy law. For the same reasons that U.S. airlines will not release information about passengers involved in airplane accidents, humanitarian relief organizations are likely to face criticism when they post on the Internet the names of people killed in natural disasters or other emergencies.

Intellectual property laws pose similar concerns. In the United States, the Clinton administration has interpreted existing copyright law as severely restricting copying, transmitting, or displaying electronic, copyrighted expression. Copyright law protects only original expression, not facts or ideas. This interpretation, however, would have the effect of extending protection to electronic data, not just the manner in which they are expressed. That interpretation is widely ignored today and justifiably criticized. But if the administration has its way, those restrictions will be clarified by Congress and the courts and be enforceable by any copyright owner whose work is infringed. In addition, as with privacy, information providers will have to contend with a wide variety of national copyright laws. Already some data posted on the Internet are accompanied by instructions forbidding access by users in listed countries, in an effort to comply with national laws that restrict access to such information.

Moreover, although the law is still unsettled in this area, some courts have extended liability concerning electronic information to parties, other than the original provider, who help provide access to it. By providing electronic links to other databases and information services, NGOs may expose themselves to liability for the conduct of others who use those resources.

Finally, we should be frank about the limits of technology. Information networks can convey words and images with great force and disseminate them more quickly, at lower cost, to a larger number of people than their printed counterparts. However, these technologies seldom improve the quality, thoughtfulness, or precision of what is communicated. The power of information technologies includes the power to mesmerize, to distract, and to substitute form for content. We should always be on our guard against that very real possibility.

Conclusion

Communications technologies, skills, and media are essential, cost-effective tools in humanitarian crisis management, prevention, mitigation, and resolution. These resources are indispensable to link scientists, relief personnel, government officials, and the public; educate the public about humanitarian crises; track approaching hazards that could result in, or contribute to, humanitarian crises; alert authorities; assess damage; collect information, supplies, and other resources; and coordinate both short- and long-term responses. Among the most important roles, as governments and NGOs are increasingly discovering, are uses of communications media and technologies to motivate public, political, and institutional responses, and to support rational policy-making and priority setting.

Each of these uses raises important issues that the humanitarian community must address. NGOs' expanding use of mass media and other means of communicating directly with the public may misinform and misfocus public attention and therefore contribute to distorting policy concerning humanitarian crises. The use of powerful new information technologies to collect real-time information about humanitarian emergencies and to link remote information resources poses even greater risks. The humanitarian community must act quickly and effectively to guarantee the authenticity and integrity of electronic data and the reliability and capacity of digital information systems. As we realize the potential of information technologies, we must ensure that both the technologies and the information they provide are available, affordable, and reliable. And our actions in this area, as in all others, must show respect for the people, cultures, and laws that they affect. The potential of the technologies involved should fuel the urgency with which we examine and resolve these issues. The failure to do so will certainly threaten our present and future capacity to use the power of communications to avert humanitarian crises and to save lives.

Notes

1. Bill Gertz and Frank Murray, "Clinton Declares Disaster in Devastated Area," *Washington Times* (January 18, 1994), A7.

2. John M. Moran, "Internet Becomes Quake-Net; Global Audience Gets Disaster Information," *Hartford Courant* (January 20, 1995), A1.

3. Bernard Cohen, *The Press and Foreign Policy* (Princeton, 1963), 13.

4. Michael R. Beschloss, "The Video Vise," *Washington Post* (May 2, 1993), C1.

5. Lawrence Wallack, "Drinking and Driving: Toward a Broader Understanding of the Role of Mass Media," *Journal of Public Health Policy,* 5 (1984), 485 (quoting a statement by George Gerbner on *Bill Moyers' Journal: TV or Not TV*, a PBS television broadcast on April 23, 1979).

6. "Quake Hits India; 1,000 Feared Dead," *New York Times* (September 30, 1993), A4.

7. Marilyn Greene and Juan J. Walte, "Quake Tragedy 'Unimaginable'; 16,000 Feared Dead in India; 10,000 Hurt," *USA Today (*October 1, 1993), 6A.

8. Edward A. Gargan, "Relief for Victims of Indian Quake Comes Slowly," *New York Times* (October 3, 1993), A3.

9. "Aid to India Quake Victims Sticks to Main Roads," *New York Times* (October 6, 1993), A11.

10. Fred H. Cate, *Media, Disaster Relief and Images of the Developing World* (Washington, D.C., 1994), 1.

11. "Public Opinion of Third World 'Grossly Distorted,' Says Aid Agency," press release from the World Vision/Research Surveys of Great Britain Omnibus Third World Perception Survey, London, October 26, 1993.

12. Peter Adamson, Address to the UNICEF National Committees, Geneva (January 29, 1991).

13. *FAO Helps Limit Disaster from Drought with Broad-Based Early Warning System and Drylands Development Strategy* (Geneva, 1994), 1.

14. Olavi Elo, address to the World Conference on Natural Disaster Reduction, Yokohama, Japan (May 1994).

15. International Federation of Red Cross and Red Crescent Societies, *World Disasters Report 1993* (Dordrecht, Netherlands, 1993), 62.

16. Adamson, address to the UNICEF National Committees.

17. *InterAction PVO Standards* (Washington, D.C., 1993), 5.3.

18. Save the Children (UK), *Focus on Images* (London, 1993), 2, 7.

19. Dale N. Hatfield, *Disaster Communications and Information Management in the International Federation of Red Cross and Red Crescent Societies: A Strategic Assessment* (Washington, D.C., 1992), 13.

20. The Internet today connects more than 45,000 separate networks and 25 million to 30 million users in more than 100 countries and is growing at the rate of 750,000 new users per month. The number of business service providers—the bellwether of future growth and expansion—on the Internet ballooned from fewer than 100 in 1990 to almost 20,000 as of late 1994.

21. At least one of the more than 150,000 Internet-based bulletin boards and discussion groups is devoted to disasters (that is, clari.news.disaster).

22. Internet address: http://www.fema.gov.

23. The Internet addresses for these organizations are: AID/OFDA (gopher://gopher.info.usaid.gov:70/1); the State of California's Governor's Office of Emergency Services (http://www.oes.ca.gov:8001/); the United Nations (gopher://gopher.undp.org:70/11/unearth); the Asian Disaster Preparedness Center (gopher://emailhost.ait.ac.th:70/11/ait.geninfo/adpc); InterAction(gopher://gopher. vita.org:70/11/intl/interaction/iact); and the Alliance for a Global Community (gopher:// gopher.vita.org:70/11/intl/interaction/alli).

24. Internet address: http://hoshi.cic.sfu.ca/~anderson.

25. Disaster Reduction Information Exchange home page, available through the Internet at http://hoshi.cic.sfu.ca/~ierris/drix.html.

26. Facility for International Readiness and Response to Emergencies home page, available through the Internet at http://hoshi.cic.sfu.ca/~ierris/firre.html.

27. Giles M. Whitcomb, *The IERRIS Project Abstract* (Geneva, 1994).

28. Internet address: http://hoshi.cic.sfu.ca/~ierris (provides a link to HazardNet as the IERRIS prototype is no longer functional).

29. An Introduction to HAZARD Net, available through the Internet at http://hoshi.cic.sfu.ca/~hazard/.

30. The Export Administration Act of 1979, Pub. L. No. 96-72, 93 Stat. 503, extended by The Export Administration Authorization for Fiscal Year 1993-94, Pub. L. No. 103-10, 107 Stat. 40 (1993), authorizes export controls "(1) [t]o protect the domestic economy from the excessive drain of scarce materials and to reduce the serious inflationary impact of foreign demand; (2) [t]o further significantly the foreign policy of the United States and to fulfill its international responsibilities; and (3) [t]o exercise the necessary vigilance over exports from the standpoint of their significance to the national security of the United States." 15 C.F.R. § 770.1(a) (1993). The Act is administered by the Bureau of Export Administration in the Department of Commerce, according to the Export Administration Regulations. 15 C.F.R. §§ 768 *et seq* (1993). Under the regulations, exporters must determine in which of a complicated series of classification categories the products to be exported fit, and then comply with the licensing requirements or restrictions applicable to that category. Although the original Act has expired, its provisions were extended temporarily by the Export Administration Authorization for Fiscal Year 1993-94, Pub. L. No. 103-10, 107 Stat. 40 (1993), pending complete revision by Congress.

The International Security Assistance and Arms Export Control Act of 1976, Pub. L. No. 94-329, 90 Stat. 729 (1976), is administered by the Department of State under the International Traffic in Arms Regulations. 22 C.F.R. §§ 120.01 *et seq* (1993). The regulations require the maintenance of a list—the United States Munitions List—containing "defense articles" and "defense services," the export and import of which are restricted or prohibited.

31. Hans Zimmerman, presentation to the Panel on Disaster Communications, International Institute of Communications 25th annual conference, Tampere, Finland, September 1994.

32.   Anne W. Branscomb, "Global Governance of Global Networks: A Survey of Transborder Data Flow in Transition," *Vanderbilt Law Review,* 36 (1983), 985, 987.

33.   Com(92)422 Final SYN 287, art. 2(a) (October 15, 1992).

34.   Louis Harris Associates and Alan F. Westin, *The Equifax Report on Consumers in the Information Age* (New York, 1993).

CHAPTER TWO

Reporting Humanitarianism:
Are the New Electronic Media
Making a Difference?

Edward R. Girardet

ARE WE ANY better informed today about the world's conflicts, human-itarian crises, or environmental disasters than we were, say, two decades ago? Has the age of the satellite dish, the Internet, and other forms of electronic media really improved our capabilities of understanding Afghanistan's continuing madness or why up to half a million people were murdered in Rwanda? Or are we simply deluding ourselves that this massive onslaught of information is indeed providing us with the sort of quality data and insight that will enable us not only to grasp what is hap-pening, but to deal more effectively with such crises?

As a journalist who has covered wars, refugee crises, and other forms of humanitarian predicaments in Africa, Asia, and other parts of the world for over fifteen years, I am not convinced that we are in any way better informed today than we were during the 1960s or 1970s. Despite having far greater access to an overwhelming surfeit of information sources than ever before, the public (and policymakers, for that matter) may not really have a more enlightened command of the humanitarian state of affairs in Angola, Afghanistan, or even the Bronx.

Attention spans are shorter and one can only absorb so much. Whether professionals or concerned members of the public, most people today simply do not have the time or patience to sift through this array of global data. Most still end up relying on a small selection of regular or proven outlets for their information: two or three television channels, a

45

newspaper, several magazines, professional reviews and newsletters perhaps, books, and one or more services on the Internet or other multimedia sources.

Even then, such diversity remains the domain of a tiny minority. The majority of Americans, and increasingly, Europeans, turn to television as their main, if not sole, source of news and current events. There is also a whole new generation of young Americans who no longer read newspapers. Obviously, such overreliance on a single and in many ways limited news outlet has a profound effect on how the public perceives humanitarian predicaments, particularly abroad.

Without seeking to explore the more evident aspects of the new electronic media and their impact on the global information highway (or network, to be more precise), I shall focus on some of the ways, both positive and negative, in which they are already affecting the coverage of humanitarian crises. Even if at times contradictory, these incorporate the ability to have both positive and negative effects:

Positive

—Broaden considerably the possibilities of global public access to information sources over which governments have little or no control. They also allow virtually anyone to communicate at little cost.

—Permit more niche programming, allowing greater specialization or detailed coverage of specific issues.

—Enable communities (including minority ethnic, tribal, religious, and political groups) to express themselves in a manner never before imaginable, not only with local but also with international counterparts elsewhere in the world.

—Improve technologically the capabilities of international newsgathering.

—Lead to greater competition among media organizations to provide more focused programming.

Negative

—Lead to a deterioration of general news programming for mainstream audiences, with major networks leaving the production of quality current events and documentary segments to niche services.

—Enable extremist political, religious, ethnic, or tribal groups to abuse niche services by catering to myths, rumor, hate, hearsay, and other forms of discrimination.

— Lead to a drop in professional journalistic standards and responsibilities. Improved technology will not necessarily encourage quality reporting as long as media coordinators remain more obsessed by the messenger than the message.

The New Media: Embracing Good with Bad

The possibilities presented by the new electronic media are overwhelming. As with any form of new technology, electronic media pose a challenge for those seeking to use their potential in a constructive and responsible manner. This includes determining some of the directions in which such forms of communication appear to be heading. It is clear, for example, that while the extraordinary diversity of these new communications' capabilities is in the process of dramatically expanding public access to information, it also threatens to restrict access by encouraging overly specialized niches that will be ignored by broader audiences.

Niche programming, for example, will prove a valuable contribution to certain sectors of society by providing a voice to minority or community interests, whether African Americans in the United States, North African Muslims in France, or Tamils in Sri Lanka. The impending arrival of cable network systems with more than 500 stations will allow greater viewing choice. At the same time, however, they will exile the majority of quality news, current affairs, and documentary programming to select channels only.

While appealing to specialized groups already interested in international (and humanitarian) affairs, such programming may never be seen by whole segments of the population, particularly younger viewers. Even CNN, which purports to be the world news channel, presents a far less cosmopolitan menu on its U.S. domestic network than the one offered globally. Although CNN began broadcasting portions of its international service to Americans at the beginning of 1995, the overall tone remains highly parochial.

According to UNICEF, recent studies indicate that young people today are far less interested in global humanitarian and development issues than they were in the past. To a concerned public, this suggests, disturbingly, that both media and educational institutions are failing to assume their responsibilities in keeping a new generation informed of what is happening in the world. Although Europeans at high school and university levels still appear to be relatively well informed about events in Bosnia or Mozambique, it is striking to note how superficial comparative awareness is among many Americans of the same age. Although saturation coverage of the Rwandas and Somalias of today will probably continue to reach general audiences, an abysmal information gap remains with regard to situations elsewhere: the plight of civilians in the conflict-ridden southern Sudan, Khmer Rouge repression in Cambodia, or slavery in the Middle East.

Part of the fault lies with editors and program directors. Many seek to appeal to what they believe to be the current public mood, without considering their purported roles within society as purveyors of credible information rather than news entertainment or diversion. "I still think that the press has a responsibility to educate and cultivate readers on issues even if they do not seem part of current trends and fashions. If editors constantly react to issues because of popularity and ratings rather than seek to go beyond, they are not doing their job," noted David Lawday, Berlin-based Central European correspondent of *The Economist*.[1]

From the humanitarian point of view, the growth of niche programming suggests that effective indicators will be needed to help guide the public toward certain channels, be they highly specific ones such as a "Human Rights Channel" or more general ones along the lines of a "World About Us," with National Geographic–type features. Yet such guidance does not look too promising. Certain types of programs containing occasional reports on refugees in southern Africa or new development initiatives in the Himalayas may obtain national prominence along the lines of the *MacNeil-Lehrer NewsHour* but will probably remain just as elitist as this program and, as a result, still fail to reach general viewers.

The problem is how to keep a general public regularly informed. Given that most network news programs in the United States normally pay little attention to humanitarian issues abroad (and when they do, it is in the form of massive onslaughts of information, to the detriment of situations elsewhere), this does not look too hopeful either. Efforts will have to be made to "educate" people in how to deal with the new media, particularly if the aim is not to lose younger viewers.

There is too little effort among high schools to teach pupils "current events" as part of their regular curriculum and to teach them how to critically "watch," "read," and otherwise interpret news sources, whether television, radio, newspapers and magazines, or the Internet. Far too much institutional funding is wasted on replicate academic exploration of issues that exclude the public (such as conferences on refugees and early warning), or in-depth reports on United Nations efficiency, which simply get shelved. Far better would be to direct resources toward more practical initiatives aimed at providing young people with incentives to understand and respond to what is happening in their world.

Media organizations such as the North American Newspaper Association or the Freedom Forum at Columbia University in New York should be seeking to work far more closely with schools to encourage current events literacy through hands-on programs. Humanitarian advocacy groups, too, should seek to become more involved. Certain niche television programs could become part of the school education process, while newspapers (which will have to embrace new approaches to keep or otherwise attract readers) should make more comprehensive efforts to join forces with schools, broadcasters, and electronic services.

There is little question that new, imaginative approaches to news education are urgently needed. If people, both young and old, are to be informed, then they will require more effective access to credible but not overwhelming information sources. This is already beginning to happen, but it still has a long way to go.

From the production point of view, a significant drawback of niche television is financial. With too many programs, there is too little money to go around. Quality television costs money. Producers, whether in North America or Europe, are finding it increasingly difficult to produce the sort of programming needed to put across the humanitarian message. Trips to Liberia, Afghanistan, or Guatemala, even in the company of relief groups willing to assist, are costly, not only because of logistics but also because of camera equipment and crews. Sending out a single journalist/cameraman (as some of the news networks are increasingly doing) with an inexpensive high-8 video may provide interesting and usable footage, particularly with regard to hard news events, but it still takes a team of two or three people to produce quality reporting.

Again, there are imaginative ways of resolving such problems, but they are not easy. Governments, foundations, sponsors, and other donors will have to make more funding available for public service programming. And this does not have to be restricted to public television networks. Pressure can be brought on commercial channels to commit a certain portion of their broadcast menus to public service information. This should include appropriate financial support and accessible airing schedules.

In Europe, a number of the commercial or mixed (that is, commercial and public service) networks make efforts to maintain relatively high standards of information and educational programming. In Britain, for example, the commercial networks are obliged by the Independent Broadcasting Authority to ensure a degree of public interest programming. Some of the best current affairs and documentary shows are often produced by the ITV networks.

Nevertheless, even the European public broadcasting networks are facing financial and editorial crunches. The amount of time apportioned to documentaries, current affairs magazines, and minority programming is dropping. As pointed out by Claire Frachon, a Paris-based producer and consultant specializing in European television trends with regard to immigrants, refugees, and other humanitarian issues, quality current affairs and documentary programming is suffering. "Broadcast commitments to humanitarian issues are going down because of competition from the commercial channels. Either the amount of such programming, including the funding, is being reduced, or quality magazine or documentary segments are being aired at absurd hours such as midnight or at seven in the morning, when most people are not watching," she said.[2]

State support (through license fees) of the European public broadcasters, such as the BBC or Germany's ARD and ZDF networks, is also in danger of being undermined by critical parliamentary and other political interests, mainly on the right. In Canada it is not much different. Facing severe cutbacks, the Canadian Broadcasting Corporation's BBC-style programming has already resulted in a distinct loss of quality public service commitment.

Although the face and format of public broadcasting will almost undoubtedly undergo major changes over the next few years in most western European countries, there is still a sufficient sense of social responsibility among the electorate to accept the need for paying for such programming. In the United States, on the other hand, the diminishing resources of public broadcasting, coupled with the current approach of the Republican party to slash such funding, do not bode well for the future.

For quality programming to exist on niche channels, broadcasters will have to pool funding resources and seek greater coproduction both at home and abroad. Producers and distributors will have to develop more imaginative approaches toward making their programming as widely available as possible. This does not necessarily have to result in a loss of quality programming. Producers should seek to avoid politically or socially correct segments that may please certain groups but are too boring for most audiences, and push for versions geared to different audiences. The same footage should be able to serve as material for broadcast on different channels in the form of traditional documentaries, news and magazine segments, children's features, clips on MTV, and so on.

Another worrisome but firmly established development threatening the quality coverage of humanitarian issues is the rise of tabloid "human interest" magazine shows, whose standards of journalistic ethics and quality have become progressively eroded in the face of commercial pressures. As producers will themselves admit, such programs have become little more than exercises in trivialization and diversion. "It's what Americans want, so we give it to them," noted one NBC producer, not without a touch of cynicism. Another senior producer with ABC added: "I am embarrassed to admit it, but we often produce junk. We can't afford to experiment with issues that we feel need to be covered but which might not attract big audiences because of the ratings. This is what network journalism has come to and it's shameful."[3]

A parallel phenomenon that has not only gripped the United States but is making itself increasingly felt in Europe is the rise of highly influential radio and television talk shows. Often aspiring to journalistic credibility by assuming current affairs formats, a few at least make the effort to present themselves as town hall discussion forums based on reported events or issues of the day. The majority, however, seem to focus on entertainment-style voyeurism. Others, such as America's right-wing *Rush Limbaugh Show*, seek to manipulate already poorly informed audiences by blithely mixing fact with massive dollops of fiction to comment on subjects ranging from foreign policy to immigration or gun control. Such programs are little better than those responsible for propagating the myths and hatred in former Yugoslavia and Rwanda or the negative image of Chechens among Russians.

Given their popularity and the relatively low production cost to both sponsors and broadcasters, however, talk shows are bound to increase. Only if the more mainstream media (such as the networks, MTV, or Fox in the United States or SAT1, SKY TV, or RTL in Europe) can be persuaded to incorporate more public service coverage of current events, and thus humanitarian issues, as part of their regular programming, can one be assured that the broader population segments will not be missed.

Another possibility is for the networks to cooperate with select niche channels to broadcast or promote portions of programs (in the way that France 2 does with France 3) to attract larger audiences. Notwithstanding the trivialization of such information programming, some producers argue that it *is* possible to offer professional, imaginative, and journalistically credible shows that appeal to wide audiences. Yet it will be up to their network chiefs (and sponsors) to give them the appropriate support.

On the surface, niche publishing or television may certainly help provide humanitarians with the sort of coverage they would like. But such ghettoization will still not guarantee them mainstream access because of viewers' practices of "zapping" and "channel surfing." Media observers will need to watch closely to see whether the public will seek its principal information from the more superficial mainstream channels and publications or whether it will turn to the various print and broadcasting niches for more detailed information.

The Internet faces a similar danger. Described by *The Economist* as a "cashless society" until now, the Internet, which serves as many as 40 million users, is now acquiring an increasingly commercial character that will threaten its hitherto public service profile. The inevitable race to commercialize the Internet is on. News organizations, foundations, universities, and other institutions should seek to ensure that an element of public service remains as part of the network.

Multimedia Journalism: Learning to Wield the Sword

In the same vein, the advent of the electronic and multimedia age in international journalism is a double-edged sword. Ranging from live television broadcasts during the Gulf War to the exchange of data via modem among human rights monitoring groups operating out of countries as far flung as Kenya, Indonesia, and Chile, such technology has opened almost unfathomable new horizons at negligible cost to a more global public. At a media workshop in March 1995 for human rights advocates, hosted by the International League for Human Rights in Geneva, the principal point of interest among participating NGOs from the developing countries was not only how to convince satellite broadcasters to cover their issues but also how to communicate with each other through the Internet.

For a long time, shortwave radio represented the most influential precursor to this brave new world of uninhibited information access. In the

1990s, shortwave radio still retains a powerful role, particularly in the third world, by allowing audiences ranging from isolated Tibetan mountain villages to crowded West African shantytowns to listen to the same outside international broadcasts. Even in the United States, certainly the country boasting the world's largest communications bazaar, BBC World Service radio broadcasts—increasingly available on local FM stations—remain for a small but growing number of Americans among the most reliable sources of general global affairs coverage.

Other forms of new media, however, are rapidly filling the breach. Until recently, the former communist governments could jam radio signals to prevent their populations from listening to forbidden outside broadcasts. Today, autocratic regimes such as those in Saudi Arabia, China, or Iran are finding that they cannot enjoy the benefits of modern communications without allowing minority (or majority) ethnic, tribal, religious, political, or generational groups to dip into the Internet or tune in to outside BBC, CNN, or MTV satellite broadcasts for news and entertainment. For the first time, hundreds of millions, if not billions, of people around the world are enjoying the freedom of access to outside information sources over which governments have no control.

Yet it is a freedom that offers no guarantees other than choice. For reasons good or bad, the electronic media lend themselves to easy exploitation by all concerned: media moguls, politicians, advertisers, dictators, editors, accountants, public relations representatives, drug cartels, lobbyists, the military, and humanitarians. For example, in a bid to control satellite television access, and thus critical information, in their own geographical sphere, the Saudis have simply brought in (or bought outright) Arabic language programs to the region. This includes financial support for the BBC Arabic language services, which, though based in Rome for ostensible reasons of independence, indicates a worrisome trend among public service broadcasters toward sponsorship that could threaten credibility.

Of course, efforts to control or otherwise manipulate information is nothing new in the history of newspaper, radio, and television. Use and abuse of the press have always existed, including the buying out of competition. The basic purpose of media—notably, to put across a message, whether for power, money, or alleged altruism—remains the same. Only the technology has changed as modes of communication have evolved from the proverbial cleftstick to carrier pigeons, cables, live radio, telexes, mobile broadcasts, faxes, cellular telephones, and desktop publishing.

News organizations, whether on the left or right, dislike being accused of manipulating information or serving interests other than their own, be they political or financial. In France, political manipulation of the broadcast networks constantly swings one way or the other—with traumatic effects on programming—depending on whether the Socialists or the Conservatives are in power. And in Germany, certain channels, such as ARD, are considered "left," while others, such as ZDF, are considered slightly more "right." But all claim to provide unadulterated information. In the United States, news organizations regularly claim to be "objective," "impartial," or "balanced" in their reporting but still come under enormous pressures from government, commercial, or establishment interests. Even in Britain, the BBC, renowned for its impartial broadcasting constitution, regularly comes under attack for presenting biased information, depending on who is running the country.

As much as the William Randolph Hearsts of the past brazenly claimed that their newspapers represented the public's right to know, the commercial networks of today like to assert, especially when criticized, that their stories represent both truth and journalistic responsibility. The fact is that the networks are just as much, if not more, obsessed with self-promotion as the former print barons were with selling newspapers and advertising. As a result, their choices of stories—whether about child prostitution in Southeast Asia or a follow-up to the crisis in Ethiopia—are becoming increasingly tied to how they will do in the ratings. Although the flogging of offenders has been a common punishment in Singapore for decades, it was only when an American youth was condemned in 1994 to six strokes for vandalism (later reduced to four) that the American media showed any interest in or outrage over the practice.

Worldwide humanitarian issues, no matter how horrific, are just as much in competition with the domestic O. J. Simpson, Amy Fisher, and John Wayne Bobbitt stories of today as they are with those international stories reflecting strong U.S. angles: the Gulf War, Somalia, and Haiti. Without U.S. strategic or other interests involved, such as American troops on foreign soil, many of these stories—be it Liberia's civil war or human rights in Burma—would never make it to the screen. "Foreign stories are not considered to have as big a rating as domestic stories so they are often simply not done," maintains Canadian filmmaker and journalist Arthur Kent. Now with the CBC's highly acclaimed documentary show, *Man Alive*, Kent resigned from NBC when the U.S. network, under pressure from its entertainment side, refused to run certain stories, such as reports on the continuing war in Afghanistan or the survivors of torture in Guatemala's civil war.

Not unlike the advent of the motor vehicle and other technological advances that have brought about radical changes in lifestyles over the past century but have also threatened the earth with pollution, the expansion of the global electronic village brings with it a Pandora's box of scourges. Goebbels's skillful use of radio (he also explored the potential of television) as a means of manipulating the German people already has its emulators. Totalitarian governments and extremist political and fundamentalist religious groups now seek to misappropriate multimedia outlets, both old and new, as a means of propagating myths, rumors, untruths, hatred, and, ultimately, terror. This, in turn, can lead to greater ghettoization, tribalism, and xenophobia, whether in the United States, South Africa, or the former Soviet Union.

One does not have to look far to behold the consequences of such information abuse. Extremist Serb and Croat minorities did much to instigate the current conflict by fueling rumor and hate through the media and creating the myth of ethnic, tribal, or religious purity in a nation where many Yugoslavs were of mixed background. Bosnians are just as much Muslim as they are Serb, Croat, or mixed.

Governments, international organizations, and humanitarian agencies regularly overlook the importance of information dissemination and the media. They are often willing to spend hundreds of millions of dollars on humanitarian or peacekeeping operations but are reluctant to allocate sufficient funding to ensure that people are properly and accurately informed. Normally, this does not take a great amount of money. Had a greater effort been made by the United Nations or the European Union, for example, to encourage more outside broadcasts in the former Yugoslavia or to provide greater support to more moderate local media, the international community might have had a better chance of helping contain the conflict.

A similar situation existed in Rwanda, another country whose now largely mixed population was artificially separated by the former colonial power's insistence on identifying individuals as either Hutu or Tutsi. The government-run Radio Milles Collines helped perpetrate this division with devastating results through its dissemination of rumor and misinformation in 1993 and 1994. While the Rwandan elites listened to shortwave broadcasts of Radio France Internationale (RFI), Deutschewelle, BBC World Service, and the Voice of America, the majority of Rwandans did not.

Only recently have organizations such as the BBC and a Swiss government–supported initiative by Reporters Sans Frontières sought to counter such propaganda by starting local radio programming of their own. And at least one lesson was learned when the U.S. authorities dropped FM radio sets in Haiti to keep the local population informed and to avoid destructive rumormongering.

New Modes of Communicating from the Field

Traditional media (notably radio, newspapers, and to a lesser extent, television) continue to assert the most news and information influence among local players in conflicts such as those in the former Yugoslavia, Somalia, Afghanistan, Angola, or Rwanda. Yet the world's lines of communication to war zones have dramatically changed in less than a decade. For all concerned—government forces, rebel groups, humanitarian organizations, traffickers, and journalists—links to the outside have been dramatically enhanced by the advent of fax machines, satellite dishes, cellular phones, laptop computers, and modems.

Before the UN/U.S. intervention in Somalia, local warlords communicated daily from their positions on both sides of Mogadishu by satellite phone and fax to their overseas representatives in Rome and London. They also commented on events directly with the BBC World Service or CNN. In Liberia, Charles Taylor, among other rebel leaders, used satellite phones driven by car batteries to deny atrocities to the BBC and to complain to UN headquarters in New York that his side was not getting its share of humanitarian relief.

At the same time, this ability to call in from the middle of nowhere allowed the chief delegate of the International Committee of the Red Cross (ICRC) in Kigali to be interviewed several times a day by the BBC, RFI, Swiss Radio International, National Public Radio, and others on the humanitarian situation in and around the capital during the worst period of the Rwandan crisis. It also enabled him to keep ICRC headquarters informed about relief requirements as soon as conditions permitted more aid to come in.

Yet we need to consider to what extent such technology will influence (and is already influencing) both the content and quality of journalism today, particularly its impact on international humanitarian issues. Have certain media gone to extreme limits, with respect to "shock content," in their efforts to portray ever more powerful imagery—notably that of decomposing bodies in Rwanda or shells exploding in the streets of Bihacs? What will be needed to galvanize world audiences when the next Somalia or Rwanda occurs? Can the international community afford to have mass coverage of one issue completely detract from the predicament of another?

The phenomenon of saturation reporting is particularly problematic for humanitarians. As many people are only too well aware, the media seem incapable of dealing with more than one issue at a time. This means that while the Rwandas of today will be covered on a massive scale before they too fade into oblivion, other crises (such as Angola, the southern Sudan, and Afghanistan) will continue to be ignored. Even Chechnya in early 1995—a brutal conflict within the Russian empire involving the indiscriminate shelling of civilians by government forces—received relatively little in-depth coverage. It also failed to prompt sufficient worldwide indignation among the donors to support appeals by the United Nations, the International Committee of the Red Cross, or Médecins Sans Frontières (MSF) for relief funds.

And in Rwanda, although a small group of foreign correspondents from newspapers ranging from *Le Monde* to the *New York Times* reported events leading up to the massacres in early 1994, it took the concept of genocide—the deliberate destruction of human life based on ethnic, racial, or religious discrimination—to convince most editors finally to cover the story. There was no question of a lack of early warning; there always is in situations such as these, whether in the form of journalist, human rights, or relief agency reports. The policy-makers failed to take heed and the editors (notably in television) refused to budge until various circumstances, including a host of reporters on their way back from the elections in South Africa, decided that they had a salable "humanitarian" story.

It is doubtful that the media would have reported on Rwanda had it "just" been a case of Rwandans killing Rwandans. Civil war–beleaguered Liberians, for example—despite their claim to being "children of America" and believing that, at least in the United States, their plight would prompt concern—found, to their distress, that their predicament rated little interest. Liberians were particularly angered by the fact that African Americans, more interested in South Africa than any other country on the continent, largely ignored them.

Various international relief agencies, notably MSF and the ICRC, were on the ground inside Monrovia as well as in the frontier regions. A sizable contingent of American and European reporters was also on the spot taking enormous risks to cover what some described as the most horrific civil war they had ever witnessed. Yet the press found that Liberians killing Liberians was just not enough to prompt any form of public outrage. Competing with the situation in the Gulf, the story scarcely made it on U.S. network television. One wonders whether Liberia would have experienced a different level of international concern had it been "blessed" with large deposits of oil rather than ravaged by horrendous human rights violations and massacres.

Why has there been such a lack of interest, not only American or European, but global? One reason is that the international community increasingly needs to justify its concern by reacting to something more morally abhorrent than the mundane killing of ordinary human beings— just as Afghans killing Afghans, Sudanese killing Sudanese, or Angolans killing Angolans is apparently insufficient to mobilize more consistent coverage.

Some international relief representatives do not consider the "outrage" factor to be a problem with regard to future coverage of new or currently ignored issues. "The public has an extraordinary capacity to demonstrate its concern as long as the information gets through," noted the director of one leading European aid agency. Other relief representatives and journalists are not so sure.

"A basic problem is that no human drama stops the moving eye any longer unless correspondents find some angle that tugs heartstrings in a new way. And each tug stretches them further. I first heard of 'compassion fatigue' in 1981; today, it is closer to compassion burnout. No people should have to endure the suffering that is now needed to get our attention,"[4] observed Mort Rosenblum of the Associated Press. According to Rosenblum, who analyses the challenges of foreign and humanitarian reporting in his latest book, *Who Stole the News?*, journalists must seek to report all calamities in a straightforward and nonsensationalist manner. This includes not only the wars and famines that the news pack decides constitute a story, but also (citing one poignant example) the 5 million Third World children who die every year for lack of simple attention. "That is as if every four minutes, all year long, a loaded school bus plunged into the Grand Canyon," adds Rosenblum.

As many journalists will agree, satellite dishes, smaller, lightweight cameras, and portable computers equipped with modems have vastly improved the logistical process of news gathering. Such technology has allowed reporters greater mobility in covering stories from Kurdistan, Cambodia, Somalia, Rwanda, and elsewhere. Television coverage of the 1979–89 Soviet-Afghan war was often grossly neglected when compared with Beirut and other conflict zones because it simply took too long—sometimes weeks—for news material to get out. Today, however, the BBC, Reuters, the Associated Press, and Agence France Presse could all offer daily reports from Kabul via portable satellite dishes.

The ability of journalists to set up mobile satellite transmitters out of a suitcase and hook up their laptops or telephones has also allowed far greater immediacy in their reporting. A journalist flying in on a United Nations transport to a remote desert landing strip besieged by refugees can transmit a story within the hour. Using on-line news services or electronic libraries, he or she can also call on reports, such as dispatches from journalists elsewhere, a newly published assessment of the situation by Human Rights Watch in New York, statistics from the United Nations High Commission for Refugees in Geneva, or a policy speech by the German Chancellor in Berlin, and incorporate them in the piece.

An Obsession with the Medium, Not the Purpose

Such technological convenience, however, threatens to seriously undermine what some in the industry still like to refer to as quality journalism and responsibility. All too often, information is confused with understanding, and high technology with journalism, so fascinated are people by the vehicle rather than the purpose.

Journalists in the field (particularly foreign correspondents) are by and large sympathetic to those involved in humanitarian plights, whether victims or relief workers. They are usually more than willing to report a situation with as many dispatches as it takes to put the issue across. It is often their editors who are not willing to allow them the necessary scope. For reasons of competition, publicity, or ratings, news organizations increasingly want to be able to claim that they have a "body" on the spot, yet they do not really care how in-depth or consistent the information is. They also want the information instantly, supported by appropriate and uncomplicated clichéd images.

This obsession with immediacy is giving journalists less time to fully research and understand the issues at hand. It encourages laziness and an overreliance on existent data. A considerable risk has already emerged of replicating mistakes and unreliable information (which gets reproduced again and again) gleaned from Nexus, CompuServe, America Online, the Internet, and other resource bases because of the temptation not to go out and do the reporting oneself.

Until recently, many foreign correspondents covering the Third World beat found that they had to rely largely on their own reporting (interviews with diplomats, relief representatives, and local sources such as farmers, dissidents, or missionaries) because other information sources (such as local newspapers) were simply not available or were considered unreliable. Today, journalists can go out armed with vast quantities of background material but may overlook interesting new angles that could provide a more perceptive grasp of the issue at hand. This discourages new insights or the breaking of fresh ground based on firsthand information.

Perhaps even more disconcerting, this confusion between technology and journalism is causing news on American television, and increasingly so on European television, to become bland, predictable in its clichés, and not particularly informative. The fact that CNN, EURONEWS, and other networks are capable of broadcasting lengthy bouts of live, unedited material from the Gulf, Somalia, Rwanda, or Haiti does not necessarily mean that the information provided will enable viewers to better understand the situation. Unedited live footage can prove exceptionally useful for those with the patience and interest to sit through long bouts of open camera, such as C-Span coverage of congressional hearings, but this should not be regarded as "reporting."

In addition, increasing attention is being given to the appearance of news reporters. The days of the rugged, rude, irreverent, chain-smoking, and shabbily dressed foreign correspondent are over. Today, the new breed of network television reporter may still be rude; but he or she is usually incredibly well dressed, coiffed, and armed with a perfect smile, yet totally removed from the situation he or she is allegedly seeking to report on for the benefit of viewers. And, in many cases, the television presenter is featured as more important than the story itself. This may be the new television, but is it journalism? Regardless of how authentic a correspondent looks wearing a flak jacket or safari outfit and standing in front of a camera, with starving children in the background or armed militia shouting slogans, physical presence does not make up for nonexistent or sloppy reporting.

This is not to say that many Western journalists failed to perform admirably once they hit the ground in Somalia, Bosnia, Rwanda, and other humanitarian crisis areas. Fortunately, there are still many television reporters and producers who consider their profession to be journalism, with the object of helping viewers understand a story, rather than news entertainment, where presentation and image are what really count.

Media coverage has contributed overwhelmingly toward attracting global attention to the issues at hand. In the case of Rwanda, it helped pressure donor governments into acting and sparked a flood of monetary support for the relief agencies. The print media certainly helped signal the situation to policy-makers, while television was probably most responsible for instigating public concern for the plight of more than 2 million civilians in the refugee camps. Some relief agencies may have complained that the press descended like vultures, but their presence was vital to maintain public support for the international relief operation. Whether television actually helped the public understand what had really happened is another matter and one that is particularly difficult, if not impossible, to determine.

As with any cottage industry, the media have their fare share of good and bad craftsmen. The press has always been slammed for sleaziness or questionable ethics—it is the most powerful institution in the United States without any form of watchdog organization of its own—but its reputation is at a noticeably low ebb. There are serious concerns both within the media and elsewhere that a growing lack of professionalism and integrity has set in, with journalists forgetting that a reporter's job is to report and not to be in the entertainment business.

Increasingly, too, many journalists have confused themselves with the story and think they are part of it, or they have grown too close to power sources. Correspondents on certain American news shows, such as CBS's *60 Minutes*, can appear in their reports more often than their subjects—sometimes more than twenty times. These correspondents are seen nodding gravely, looking extremely concerned, or they are seen standing in neatly pressed combat or safari gear among starving children, when there is no plausible reason to do so other than to gain public exposure themselves. Such pretentiousness is little more than journalistic entertainment and often an insult to their subjects.

Similarly, there is a growing tendency among certain journalists to consider themselves key players, even judges, in policy-making. It is disturbing to note how palsy-walsy many journalists, fascinated by their own self-importance, have become with high political officials in Washington. On first-name terms with politicians, invited to the same functions as they are, and heralded as stars, some journalists are now part of the same club when they should instead be cultivating a critical distance. This leads to a lack of credibility and is not the role of journalists. Even the highly prestigious current affairs program *The MacNeil-Lehrer NewsHour* is in danger of becoming too Washington-oriented and has been losing many of its once faithful viewers nationwide.

At the same time, this raises an uncomfortable question for humanitarianism. Many journalists (including this writer) rely heavily on close cooperation with international relief agencies for their coverage. This is because it is often impossible for a journalist to operate in the field without their assistance. In many situations, such as during the Ethiopian, Somali, or Mozambican emergencies, journalists rely on the agencies for in-country travel, accommodation, food, contacts, and help in obtaining permits. Visiting correspondents from the outside often have difficulty renting a vehicle or even buying gasoline. Very often, too, relief agencies are the only ones with appropriate access to crisis areas such as refugee camps.

What this implies, of course, is that journalists risk becoming overly dependent on international relief agencies—all of which, like Washington politicians, have their own agendas—for their reporting. There are certainly agencies that like to push their own activities rather than the overall issue by hoarding their "own" journalists. These agencies seek to ensure that visiting reporters cover as much as possible in the company of their own relief workers.

Other journalists, while operating with the relief agencies, make efforts to interview and travel with different groups to obtain a broader and less partisan picture. There is little doubt that humanitarian field organizations perform a vital role in assisting journalists in their coverage. Reporters, however, must still be aware that one of their prime responsibilities is to get the story out without being too beholden to one particular agency, guerrilla organization, government office.

Although journalists certainly exert a major influence in providing the sort of information required for policy-making, many tend to forget that it is their reporting that is required, not their personalities. Journalists as human beings, or stars, are completely dispensable. As journalist and writer Ed Behr states in his book, *Anyone Here Been Raped and Speaks English?*, governments, guerrilla factions, relief agencies, or lobbying groups talk to journalists not because journalists are nice people, but because the press represents a means of communicating to a larger audience.[5] It does not even matter who the journalistic intermediary is; once journalists no longer serve the purpose, they are out.

This was strikingly evident during the Gulf War. As correspondents and producers who have covered conflicts in Afghanistan, Cambodia, or the Horn of Africa have pointed out, the Gulf situation was probably the most shameful episode to date of modern technology journalism. More than 3,000 journalists, cameramen, technicians, photographers, and aides converged on the Middle East as part of one huge circus. Yet the information they provided—despite all their satellite links, live reports, and gameboard electronics—was far less comprehensive and reliable than the reporting produced out of Vietnam or even Afghanistan.

Although some correspondents sought to maintain professional standards, many editors and journalists seemed to forget what basic reporting was all about. They eagerly went to bed with their governments and became incredulously obsessed by the electronic and entertainment aspects of their coverage. As some veteran correspondents pointed out, it was extraordinary how gullible many of the "fly-ins" from New York, Washington, London, or Paris, with little or no experience in war reporting, were.

This was not sour grapes. It was the fact that the entire Gulf coverage had become part of a television game, with the so-called "surgical war" well-removed from the human element. War reporting was in vogue, and technologically luxurious, but it had little to do with what was really going on. Many journalists did not know whether what they were reporting was accurate or not, but it looked good because it was "live." Many, too, also referred to the Allied side as "us" and the Iraqis as "them"—not a very professional way to report a war.

The editorial head offices knew what they wanted because they had received off-the-record, "in-depth" briefings by their governments, whether American, French, or British. Many did not want their experienced correspondents on the ground to ruin this picture with nagging questions about what was really going on. As a result, the Gulf War became a media farce manipulated as much by the U.S. and Allied military as by the regime of Saddam Hussein. For journalists to accept such a situation, as many did, was inexcusable.

The Gulf War phenomenon has significantly affected coverage in other parts of the world, notably humanitarian crises such as those in

Somalia, Rwanda, and, to a point, Chechnya. The new technology enables outside television or news teams, particularly so-called "talent squads" (or local or national television stars), to fly in and fly out on short notice from New York, London, or Paris to "do" live programs from the field. Yet many are not willing to undertake the sort of nitty-gritty legwork needed to explain what is really happening.

As any experienced relief worker or journalist can attest, it can take days, if not weeks, to feel one's way into a operation. Outsiders parachuted in with no experience of such issues have little or no gut feeling about the situation, or they seek to assess events according to their own values without paying attention to local culture or traditions.

This can lead to gross misrepresentations of events on the ground. During the Rwanda crisis, some reporters persisted in describing the outbreak of cholera as part of the "genocide" rather than a fact of life (easily prevented with proper intervention) when enormous numbers of people are obliged to live in unsanitary conditions. For Alain Destexhe, member of the Belgian Senate and former secretary general of MSF-International in Brussels, the nonsense of such imagery threatened "to efface the realities of genocide inside Rwanda."

Even more disconcerting, there is a tendency to arrive with totally preconceived notions of what the story is about. Far too much credence among both editors and journalists is lent to sources well removed from the realities on the ground, such as government officials or policy experts back in Europe or North America. This also includes their relying too much on convenient contacts, such as U.S. military spokesmen in Five O'Clock Folly–type press conferences, rather than talking to a wider array of possible sources ranging from relief organizations to local populations.

All too often, there are instances of live television coverage from Kurdistan, the Gulf War, or Haiti, with reporters commenting on events about which they are ill informed. Much of it is superficial. This, in turn, leads toward even more guessformation and infotainment masquerading as journalism. The public would be far better served by a 90-second television segment or a 600-word newspaper dispatch based on a solid day's reporting than listening to someone comment live for long periods at a time on what may or may not be occurring in front of the camera.

The fact that journalists are simply not taking the time (or are not allowed by their organizations to take the time) to undertake the sort of background digging necessary is reflected in their reporting. But their coverage is still passed off as credible news. Or they rely on visual grue-someness—the bodies of Rwandan civilians lying in a ditch, a whimper-ing Somali child lying next to its dead mother, a crowd beating up a sus-pected government informer in Haiti—to put the message across.

The persistence of certain media to delve further into meaningless clichés contributes little toward conveying the real story. One good example of this was the media's predilection during the earlier stages of the Somalia crisis to report the story as being largely the result of an Ethiopian-style famine. Many editors, both in Europe and North America, seemed reluctant to provide coverage for "just another African war" in a country whose formerly nomadic population had grown to the extent that they could no longer support themselves without foreign aid, and where greedy warlords were pursuing a ruthless power struggle at the cost of their own people.

"Little of the news coverage of Somalia dealt with that state of affairs, or the moral dilemma that it posed for western donors. Instead, the public was subjected to an unending stream of images and horror with little explanation of what anyone could actually do to change it," commented William Dowell of *Time* magazine.[6]

As organizations such as UNICEF, Oxfam, and the Federation of Red Cross Societies observe, it is generally understood among the interna-tional relief community that the media need to simplify issues. Never-theless, they note that journalists often fail to help their audiences really understand the reasons behind such conflicts and other humanitarian predicaments.

Improving the Quality of Humanitarian Reporting

Most professionals concerned with the role of the media in interna-tional humanitarian reporting are aware of the drawbacks with regard to such coverage. New technology alone will not improve the quality of data despite the alleged potential of the information highway. Neither will more conferences or symposia contribute much toward remedying such inadequacies.

What is needed are more practical ways of persuading those responsi-ble for information gathering—editors, producers, network directors, database coordinators—to provide the sort of coverage that will enable both specialized and general audiences to better understand the issues at hand. This means providing more than saturated or sensationalist one-off coverage of humanitarian crises such as Rwanda; it means providing consistent, straight reporting of critical issues worldwide. It also means encouraging greater professional integrity among the major media through the way stories are reported and presented.

The recent creation of the International Centre for Humanitarian Reporting (ICHR) by journalists, relief professionals, and concerned citizens is one such effort aimed at the improving the quality of coverage of neglected humanitarian issues.[7] The ICHR seeks to develop closer cooperation between the international media, aid organizations, the business community, and policy-makers by promoting a more hands-on approach: media grants to help cover the costs of reporting of humanitarian crises and development issues, contacts for coproduction arrangements, information workshops for both journalists and aid representatives, and an international television festival on war and humanitarian reporting.

Another initiative is the soon-to-be established International Centre for the Communication of Global Development and Humanitarian Issues, a research institution that seeks to provide advisory and information services to those involved in the communication of such issues. It will also aim to promote quality coverage by encouraging dialogue between research institutes, aid organizations in industrial and Third World countries, and members of the media.

My own news journal, *CROSSLINES Global Report*, is edited and reported by an international network of journalists, editors, and producers interested in humanitarian issues. Aimed not only at aid professionals and the media but also at other areas such as human rights, the military, and the private sector, it seeks to provide pointers and background information on international relief action and other world trends.

Given the rising costs of the reporting of humanitarian issues, a more rational approach is needed to improve the quality and accessibility of such coverage. This includes creating more imaginative forms of international coproduction and resource sharing among print, broadcast, and other media. It also includes making greater use of a broad global network of mainly freelance journalists with a good knowledge of the countries and regions in which they operate. These could assist broadcast and other news organizations with credible reporting expertise, particularly during crisis situations.

The media have the technological means to provide the quality reporting of international humanitarian issues that is lacking in so many areas. They also have the means to reach the global audiences, both general and specialized, that would benefit from such coverage. Despite the many important advances now possible in this new electronic age, nothing yet has managed to replace the basic concept of responsible journalism and the editorial will to provide the sort of information that is needed.

Notes

1. Interview with David Lawday, November 1995.
2. Claire Frachon's *Television d'Europe et Immigration* (Paris, 1993), a book exploring how immigration issues are dealt with by European television networks, was published by the Institut National de l'Audiovisual and the Association Dialogue Entre Les Cultures.
3. In interviews with television producers. Names available from the author.
4 Mort Rosenblum, *Who Stole the News? Why We Can't Keep Up With What Happens in the World and What We Can Do About It* (New York, 1993).
5. Edward Behr, *Anyone Here Been Raped and Speaks English? A Foreign Correspondent's Life behind the Lines* (London, 1992).
6. William T. Dowell, who is currently a *Time* reporter, explores this issue in an essay, "Reporting the Wars," in *Somalia, Rwanda and Beyond—The Role of the International Media in Wars and Humanitarian Crises* (New York, 1995).
7. The International Centre for Humanitarian Reporting (ICHR) is a non-governmental organization based in Geneva, Switzerland, with a support office in Cambridge, Massachusetts. Its international advisory board consists of representatives from the media, the relief community, and the private sector.

CHAPTER THREE

Suffering in Silence:
Media Coverage of War and
Famine in the Sudan

Steven Livingston

IN CONTEMPORARY world politics, the media are important, though sometimes fickle players, lavishing attention on some crises while ignoring others. Bosnia falls in the first category, while the carnage in Afghanistan, Nagorno-Karabakh, Kashmir, and Angola, to name but a few areas, falls in the latter.

Why do some situations become the object of intense news scrutiny while others of an exact or similar nature remain obscure? What makes for a newsworthy humanitarian affairs story? If we can address these and related questions, we may also come to understand how to assist the news media in covering humanitarian crises. The place to begin is with a careful analysis of the key factors in news decision-making.

Gatekeeping and News Decision-Making

Gatekeeping in communication theory is the process by which a nearly infinite array of possible news items is narrowed to the relative handful actually transmitted by the media and heard, read, or seen by audiences.[1] Some messages are prominently displayed, facilitating low-cost public consumption, while others remain obscure or altogether absent.[2]

As a theoretical construct applied to social phenomena, gatekeeping studies got their start nearly fifty years ago with the work of Lewin.[3]

Lewin was interested in developing a more complete understanding of the social forces that account for change and social choice. To conceptualize this process, he relied on the metaphor of channels, gates, and force.

A channel is simply the route, constructed temporally and often geographically, of a decision-making process. With the example of food consumption, at multiple points along a channel, decisions are made regarding what to buy or grow, what to weed out of the garden, or what to leave behind in the grocery store. In the home, additional points along the channel determine whether the food will be stored for later use or consumed immediately. Furthermore, some of the food is changed (flour made into bread, eggs into omelets), which also involves choice.[4]

This general theoretical framework, Lewin believed, was applicable to a wide variety of social situations, including news decision-making. "This situation," said Lewin, "holds not only for food channels but also for the traveling of a news item through certain communication channels."[5]

Each decision point along the channel constitutes a gate, a point at which some news item will either be excluded from the channel, initially collected only to be discarded later, or promptly passed through various gates and into the news. Progress in the channel is controlled by a series of gatekeepers—the journalists, editors, and others who make the key decisions affecting a story. Gates, then, are decision and action points that interconnect and interact with other channels and gatekeepers.

In 1949, David Manning White, a former research assistant of Lewin's, applied these ideas to how news makes its way to the public. He compared the wire service copy available to the editor of a midsize midwestern city with what was actually published over a one-week period. He found that only about 10 percent of the total available to the editor, whom White referred to as "Mr. Gates," was actually used.

Mr. Gates provided White with written explanations of why particular stories were rejected. White concluded that about one-third of the time the editor rejected stories solely on his appraisal of the merit of their newsworthiness. The remaining two-thirds of the items were rejected because of space limitations or repetition of recently run stories.

White's model was developed in subsequent research to take account of the multitude of potential gatekeepers any news story must traverse in order to reach an audience. By the late 1960s and 1970s, researchers began debating the relative importance of various gatekeepers. Halloran, Elliott, and Murdock, for instance, argued that gatekeeping began further back in the channel, well before a news story reached the editorial office (the news processors), or even the transmission point.[6] The first gate-keeper is the reporter on the street (the newsgatherer), selecting some stories and not others.

Most of the raw data used to construct news accounts come not from direct journalist exposure to an event but from sources, usually govern-ment authorities. Most of the power to define reality, in this view of the news process, resides at the point of the reporter-source contact. By the time the story makes its way to the editor, the most important gatekeep-ing decisions have already been made. The factors that impede or, con-versely, encourage reporter interaction with some sources and events and not others are important for understanding news content.

Finally, different forces are also at play in the decision-making process along the channel. Monetary expenditure is one. Time is another. The cost of obtaining a particular news item (its remoteness, the danger involved in covering it, and any lack of direct national involvement) may cause a journalist or an editor to be reluctant to invest in the progress of the story along the news channel. However, should the story progress beyond these initial gates, once through the gate, "cost" is converted to an "investment" to be recouped by filling the newshole. It may even be given special treatment, such as being the lead story. More time and space may then also be devoted to it.

This model has served as one of the basic research tools used in polit-ical communication research.[7] For our purposes, it is a relatively straight-forward and useful tool for understanding news selection. As Shoemaker has noted in reviewing the vast gatekeeping research literature, most ana-lysts agree on those factors that seem to explain news selection best.[8] Among the factors typically listed (and those used to structure this analy-sis) are proximity, uniqueness, and relevance to local or national interest.

I use the gatekeeping framework to analyze the news content—or the lack thereof—of the Sudan, one pressing humanitarian situation. As a point of comparison, I also discuss media coverage of the war and famine in Somalia. Although such a comparison may not be entirely generaliz-able to other regions in the world, it will speak to news coverage in Africa.

Somalia and the Sudan: Similarities and Contrasts

In 1992, Andrew Natsios, then head of overseas relief for the United States Agency for International Development (USAID), described

Somalia as "the most acute humanitarian tragedy in the world today."[9] American network news and newspapers reinforced the point with heartrending images of starving Somalis. The United Nations and the International Committee for the Red Cross estimated that 300,000 to 500,000 people had died as a consequence of war, famine, and disease. To escape from these conditions, 1 million Somalis had fled the country, with another 2 million being internally displaced.[10] As the gripping pictures on American television screens suggested, the horrible conditions in Somalia deserved world attention.

But Somalia was not alone. In Angola, the United Nations estimated that 1,000 people were being killed each day by the combined effects of war, hunger, and disease.[11] At about the same time, Somalia's neighbor, the Sudan, continued to suffer misery as profound as any found on the continent. Yet, for the most part, it suffered without American media attention.

For twenty-eight of the past thirty-eight years, civil war has pitted the Khartoum government—dominated by the northern Sudan's Muslim, largely Arab population—against rebels from the predominantly black Christian and animist South. In the past decade, war, drought, and famine have taken a horrible human toll. In some parts of the Sudan, malnutrition rates have been "among the highest ever documented," according to the U.S. Centers for Disease Control.[12] At the beginning of 1994, 1.5 million people were at risk of starvation.[13] There were also nearly 400,000 Sudanese refugees in neighboring countries, with another 4 million "internally displaced" people forced to flee their homes. In 1992 alone, 1 million civilians were displaced as government forces from the North captured several towns previously held by the Sudanese People's Liberation Army (SPLA).[14]

The Sudanese army, however, was not the only source of misery for the civilian population in the South. By 1994, fighting between rival factions of the SPLA cleaved along tribal and clan lines was, in the view of the UN, "the main cause of famine and displacement" among those in the south.[15] According to the United States Committee for Refugees (USCR), from 1992 to mid-1993, 300,000 people died in the southern Sudan as a result of war and war-related famine.[16] These conditions, measured statistically, rivaled those in Somalia.

Yet the southern Sudan, unlike Somalia, has been largely ignored by the American media. In 1992, Jennifer Parmelee of the *Washington Post* offered this assessment: "While the wars in Somalia and Yugoslavia have

gained a high international profile, Sudan has won almost no attention."[17] Two years later, Parmelee repeated that the war in the Sudan
"continues apace, virtually ignored by the outside world, without any of
the attention devoted to the nearby Somali disaster, slipping only occa-
sionally into world view when Khartoum is accused of supporting ter-
rorists."[18]

The Sudan has been the forgotten war. Why has the Sudan, a country
that has experienced so much misery, been largely ignored by the
Western press corps? As a point of comparison, why did similar conditions in Somalia during the same time period become the focus of an outpouring of attention and aid?

A comparison of Somalia and the Sudan offers something of a natural
experimental setting for at least three reasons. At the most general level,
both countries are ignored most of the time by the Western press. One of
the aphorisms of media reporting is that the death of a single Westerner
is treated in the same manner as the death of dozens, hundreds, or even
thousands of non-Westerners. The media ignore, for better or worse,
wide swaths of the earth. Coverage of disasters, death, and destruction is
weighed according to the location—and perhaps the race and ethnicity—
of the victims. Comparison of Somalia's coverage with that of the Sudan
holds this factor constant.

Second, besides race and regionalism, one other factor that influences
general trends in media coverage is the foreign policy orientation of the
United States. The American news media tend to focus on those foreign
problems that have been the focus of Washington's attention.[19]

Francis Deng, senior fellow at the Brookings Institution and former
ambassador and foreign minister of the Sudan, put it this way:

> Media reflect the fundamental policy orientation of a country.
> Therefore, we should ask what the American perspective is on the
> Sudan. In that perspective, though the Sudan is one of those Africa
> countries that is both African and Arab, it is seen as more of a
> Middle Eastern country.
>
> Though post–Cold War foreign policy may not be clear, Middle
> East policy is: Protect Israel and oil and isolate (Islamic) funda-
> mentalism. The South, then, becomes more remote. It is a humani-
> tarian crisis, but nothing more. The strategic interests of the United
> States' focus are on the north's "Arabness," which marginalizes the
> south.[20]

Neither the Sudan nor Somalia is of significant strategic concern to Washington in the post–Cold War era. Differences in news coverage of either country are thus not explained by differing geopolitical considerations.

Third, in large measure both countries are covered by the same Nairobi-based press corps. With the same correspondents responsible for covering both the Sudan and Somalia, factors unique to the personality traits and predilections of individual reporters and differences in news bureau funding and staffing are held constant.[21]

For these reasons, the comparison of American news coverage of the Sudan and Somalia offers a unique opportunity to understand news media decision-making processes.

An Initial Quantitative Description

All *Washington Post* articles regarding the Sudan for an eleven-year period beginning in 1983 and ending in October 1994 were obtained from Mead Data Central's Nexis system and coded, as were all *Post* stories about Somalia from 1990 to October 1994. The difference in scale reflects the respective duration of civil unrest and intermittent drought and famine in each country. The *Washington Post* was selected for detailed analysis because of its stature and commitment to international news.

Figure 1 shows trend lines for *Post* coverage of the Sudan and Somalia over an extended period. Figure 2 focuses more closely on the 1990–94 time period. What is most striking is the relative paucity of attention paid to either country. The high mark for the Sudanese conflict is 1985. In April of that year, the Sudan's president, Gaafar Nimeri, was overthrown by the military, a development that was regarded as a setback for American foreign policy. A supporter of the Camp David Accords and a staunch opponent of Libya, Nimeri had been a longtime friend of the United States. Another government shake-up occurred in March 1989, when Prime Minister Sadiq el Mahdi resigned to allow for the formation of a government of national reconciliation.

In 1991, we see a stunning increase in stories about Somalia. There is also another sharp increase in stories toward the end of 1992, explained largely by the introduction of U.S. troops by the Bush administration. The apex is the October battle in Mogadishu, which saw the death of nearly 300 Somalis and eighteen American soldiers.

FIGURE 1. *Washington Post* Articles with Primary Focus on the Sudan and Somalia, 1983–94

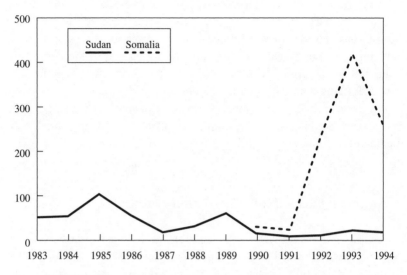

SOURCE: Author's calculations.

Turning to the Sudan, despite a government offensive in the South and the severe deterioration in conditions, the *Post* paid scant attention. Some 300,000 persons perished from 1992 to October 1993. Although there was a slight increase in coverage between 1992 and 1993, many of these stories reflect what Deng refers to as the American view of the Sudan as an Arab or Middle Eastern story, emphasizing the Sudan's involvement in terrorism.

These data raise interesting questions about the coverage of these two tragic situations. Most intriguing of all is: Why did the Sudan suffer in relative silence year after year, while Somalia, at least for a time, was the focus of intense media attention?

In brief, what are the "gates" encountered by those interested in telling the Sudan's story? They include logistics, legal impediments, safety, and news attention cycles.

Logistics

At nearly 1 million square miles, the entire Sudan is about the size of western Europe. A familiar comparison for the southern portion is to say it is about the size of France.

FIGURE 2. *Washington Post* Articles with Primary Focus on the Sudan and Somalia, 1990-92

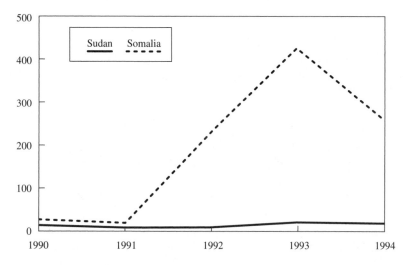

SOURCE: Author's calculations.

Travel in the southern Sudan is difficult in the best of times and impossible during the rainy season, when what few roads there are become impassable. The war also makes overland travel hazardous. Costly air travel is often the only reliable method.

Writing in the *Washington Post* in 1986, correspondent Blaine Harden described one of his trips into the southern Sudan:

> It was to have been the journalistic equivalent of a surgical strike. We would zip into rebel-held Sudan late Monday, grab an interview with the seldom-seen rebel boss, John Garang, and zip out again Thursday. All this, with plenty of time to write a nice weekend piece.
>
> It did not work. We of the international press, with our imperious expectations and our all-important deadlines, had not reckoned with the character of Sudan, a 30-year-old country that has known 20 years of civil war. Once one steps off an airplane in southern Sudan, one zips nowhere.
>
> Our surgical strike stretched into a seven-day tutorial on African guerrilla warfare. The course came complete with dizzying hunger,

six bug-slapping days in the 100-degree sun, a major tropical storm and a water supply usually reserved for lions. . . .

Toward the end, we feared—and for a few hunger-benighted moments even hoped—that we would die.[22]

The long flight north from Nairobi to Lokichokio, the UN base camp in northern Kenya, is often marked by delays, sometimes of several hours. An entire day may be spent merely getting to Lokichokio, which is itself but a staging area for travel to destinations in the Sudan.

Besides travel delays, there are other difficulties. The UN camp lacks a trained press officer. This means considerable time is spent by the visiting journalist on matters other than getting the story, such as arranging accommodations at Lokichokio and transportation to specific locations in the Sudan.

Another difficulty is communication from Lokichokio. A satellite phone/fax works only intermittently, and the only other means of communication is two-way radio. This means that once a reporter has a story from the Sudan, he or she must wait for a return flight to Nairobi before filing it.

When asked why there was coverage of Somalia but not the Sudan, Reid Miller, Nairobi bureau chief for the Associated Press (AP), put it this way: "Sudan is a very, very difficult place to cover. Somalia was easy." When pressed to provide specifics, he said:

> Well, for one thing, size. We had famine in a relatively limited area in Somalia. And it was easy to get to. Sudan is vast. The south of Sudan is bigger than France. Roads are almost nonexistent. Telephones aren't there. To get from place to place you have to charter a plane or fly with an aid agency. The aid agencies are reluctant to take journalists because of their deals with Khartoum. So it becomes a very expensive proposition.
>
> We have chartered [aircraft] individually, we have shared charters with other news organizations. But getting around that country is incredibly, incredibly difficult. And during the rainy season the few dirt strips that serve some communities are unusable. Roads get washed out. You can't travel overland.[23]

Parmelee, of the *Washington Post*, began a recent article on the situation in the Sudan by answering the implicit question of why there was so little coverage of the country. "One reason," she responded, "is that the south is largely inaccessible; this reporter flew in with aid workers and traveled the region with them by car."[24]

Robert Press of the *Christian Science Monitor*, who, after nine years in Nairobi, is one of the senior Western correspondents in East Africa, also put the travel factor at the top of his list. "With Somalia, at nine in the morning I could catch a plane at the airport here in Nairobi and make it up to Mogadishu in time to spend two or three hours on the ground and still make it back in time for dinner. In the Sudan, I've got to be able to put aside three or four days to get a story. It's just much more of a commitment."[25]

Parmelee added another important consideration, the fact that the suffering in Somalia was great but was also concentrated in a limited geographical area: "It's in part explained by the sheer numbers who were able to die in front of your camera."[26] The famine in Somalia was both severe *and* concentrated in a relatively manageable geographical area easily reached by air transportation. In the Sudan, on the other hand, "there are pockets of suffering spread out over great distances. This makes it difficult to cover, particularly for television."[27]

In a recent critique of media coverage of famines, Michael Maren writes, "In Somalia I had seen day-trippers—the camera crews that bounded off relief planes and asked the nearest relief worker to take them to the sickest children before the plane took off again in 30 minutes. The relief workers usually obliged."[28] In the Sudan, both relief workers and the Sudanese are quite media savvy. Clusters of people form upon the arrival of a Westerner, with the older men pushing forward the more malnourished of the group, often children. The SPLA guerrillas, who themselves tend to be relatively well fed, sometimes instruct the people to arrange themselves differently for better photographic effect.

Somalia was an easier story. There, specifically in Mogadishu, "we had facilities at our disposal that we don't have in Sudan," said Reid Miller of the Associated Press.

> We could fly into Mogadishu, or any one of the several cities in the south where the famine was, with relative ease. *The UN took us in at no cost.* At the drop of a hat you could be there. That sort of situation just does not exist in Sudan. It [Somalia] was a limited geographical area and we had ready access.[29]

The same point is recognized by American officials in Khartoum, Nairobi, and Washington. Donald Petterson, the United States ambassador in Khartoum, stated in an interview that on several occasions he had tried organizing more press coverage, but to no avail. "The logistics are difficult. Adding to the difficulty is the fact that the story isn't a constant drama. Something awful happens and then maybe they'll cover it. But a sustained story is difficult when the war goes on year after year."[30]

Because of its size and underdevelopment, the Sudan is, in the words of Megan Hill, the East Africa desk officer for USAID, a logistical nightmare, "particularly for the television crews."[31] Ann Stingle, external communication associate for the Red Cross and the person often credited for bringing the situation in Somalia to the attention of the Western press, agrees that covering Somalia was relatively easy. She organized some of the early press forays into Mogadishu. "We could provide the transportation and hire the security. It's entirely different in Sudan."[32]

Staffing in news bureaus in Nairobi compounds the problem. Most bureaus, even for the major news organizations, have just one reporter. Only the wire services have the relative luxury of staffing with more than one correspondent. "Both Keith [Richburg] and I spent a lot of time in Somalia last year," said Miller.

> But I had other people available to go elsewhere. As long as Keith was in Somalia he couldn't get to some of these other places. Try as he might, work as hard as he might—and he does work hard—there are certain limitations. We cover eleven countries in East Africa and the Horn. Only a small part of Africa. Yet our territory alone is a big as the United States east of the Mississippi. It's a huge territory.[33]

Richburg himself emphasized the same point. While sitting in his office in Nairobi, noodling a fistful of open-ended, prepurchased airline tickets for destinations all over East Africa, he pointed out that he could not cover everything. "It's just more than a single person can manage."[34]

Gary Strieker of CNN perhaps best illustrates the point. Normally based in Nairobi, Strieker was in either Rwanda, Tanzania, or Uganda for much of a two-month period in early 1994. As the only CNN correspondent based in that part of Africa, he constantly lives out of a backpack.

By June 1994, several months after her arrival at the Nairobi bureau, the *New York Times*'s Donatella Lorch had not had the time to go anywhere but Somalia and Rwanda. When asked about the impediments to reporting from Africa, she emphasized the distances and logistical difficulties. "Logistics is daunting in Africa. Editors back in New York don't realize this. They have preconceived notions that things can be done in Africa like in other places." [35]

Although certainly not the entire explanation, a large part of the difference between reporting from the Sudan and Somalia has to do with logistical difficulties. Nearly all of those interviewed, whether they were reporters or officials, raised the issue of geographical size, distance, and the underdevelopment of the region that make travel so difficult. Probably more than any other single factor, underdevelopment stands as a hindrance to more thorough coverage of the war and famine in the southern Sudan.

How generalizable is this factor? It seems logical to assume that similar gates stand in the way of reporting elsewhere in Africa. Angola, for example, is usually covered by news bureaus in Johannesburg, South Africa. The distances involved in traveling to Angola from there are similar to those found between Nairobi and points in the southern Sudan. What is more, after a generation of war, conditions in parts of Angola are as ravaged and dangerous as those in the Sudan. In short, the same general reporting obstacles found for the southern Sudan are also found elsewhere in Africa, with similar effect.

Legal Impediments

Legal difficulties offer another significant obstacle. The weight of the law is probably felt most heavily by the local press. In Kenya, for example, the legal system has been used in what critics have called a campaign against the press. According to Thomas Dowling, information officer at the American Embassy in Nairobi, the Kenyan government's "technique is to actually use the courts to harass or cripple the alternative press."[36]

In the past few years, greater press restrictions have become evident elsewhere in Africa. Besides being jailed and fined, journalists have been beaten and in some cases even killed. In Zambia in 1994, editors of the critical *Weekly Post* faced jail terms. In Nigeria, newspapers were routinely closed and journalists jailed. In Uganda, also in 1994, President Yoweri Museveni sponsored a media bill that would license reporters and establish a government complaints commission that would have the authority to suspend them.

Foreign journalists trying to cover Africa are also subject to the sometimes arbitrary enforcement of laws. In 1994, for example, Kenyan immigration officials arrested the pregnant wife of an American correspondent who covered east Africa for the *London Daily Telegraph*. That correspondent, Scott Peterson, characterized his wife's arrest as a part of a campaign of harassment against the foreign press. He said he had been accredited as a journalist by the Information Ministry in 1992, but that his accreditation had been withdrawn by the government in 1994, in protest against what it called his "unacceptable" news coverage of Kenya.[37]

Even gaining access to some countries is a problem when restrictions on entry are used to prevent unfavorable coverage. In 1983, for instance, Angola, Botswana, Mozambique, Tanzania, Zambia, and Zimbabwe all imposed strict foreign press controls, including censorship, on news coverage. Zimbabwe immediately used the ban to expel British and German television crews.[38]

In white-ruled South Africa, foreign press restrictions began in November 1985, with the ban on photographs (including video and film) and sound recordings of violence. In June 1986, these restrictions were expanded to include print coverage. The principal objective of the restrictions, of course, was to keep antiapartheid conflicts off European and American television. As the *New York Times* reported some months later, the measures proved quite effective.[39] According to the *Times*'s own tabulation, in June 1986 it published forty-five articles (sixteen on page one) with South African datelines. By January 1987, following the imposition of the restrictions, it published twenty-four articles (one on page one). Similarly, the *Washington Post* carried thirty-five articles with South Africa datelines in June 1986 (twenty-three on page one) and twenty in January 1987 (one on page one). Television coverage followed the same pattern.[40]

The risk of expulsion put teeth in the restrictions. In January 1987, South African authorities forced Alan Cowell, the bureau chief of the *New York Times*, to leave the country; they then refused to issue a visa to his designated successor.

Though apartheid has ended in South Africa, press restrictions are still common elsewhere in Africa. "Here if something blows up in say Burundi . . . if you don't have a visa you may have to spend a day or two getting one. And then you have to find a way of getting there," remarked the AP's Terry Leonard. "This is very, very difficult."[41] In Somalia in 1992, of course, as many journalists point out, visas were not a problem, for there was no government to require them.

In the Sudan, the issue of national sovereignty is much more prob-lematic. Despite recent actions elsewhere, the United States lacks the will to enforce UN resolutions regarding the southern Sudan. As has been made clear in interviews by Ambassador Petterson, presidential advisor Don Steinberg, and others in the State Department, Washington is not prepared to establish safe zones or any other similar arrangement in the southern Sudan. Without the backing of Western military powers, the position of the UN and NGOs in the South is tenuous. Deng and Minear point out that the government in the Sudan has mixed feelings about the aid in the first place:

> While expressing gratitude for the aid received, the Khartoum authorities were acutely conscious of its origins in the Christian West and of its delivery by a host of Christian nongovernmental organizations, some committed to spreading their religious faith as well as to saving lives.[42]

Aid not only feeds the hungry, it is also a source of humiliation for the Sudanese government. The existence of outside aid implies that Khar-toum is incapable of providing for the well-being of its own citizens. "These issues not only touch on the central values of sovereignty but also go to the heart of the national purpose and legitimacy of the govern-ment."[43] An increase in Western news attention to the southern Sudan may potentially have mixed consequences. On the one hand, more media attention may well lead to an increase in donor attention. On the other hand, it may also antagonize the already sensitive feelings of the Khar-toum government, thus threatening the entire relief program. And without a more robust U.S. or UN policy, such as the establishment of military exclusion zone(s), Operation LifeLine Sudan (OLS) remains at the mercy of the Khartoum government. Before assuming that increased media attention is necessarily positive, the potential political conse-quences must be carefully evaluated. Deng raised this same issue. "There is a feeling in Washington that should the West side too closely with the South, it would only antagonize the Muslim world."[44] In short, OLS must continue to walk a fine line regarding media coverage so as not to cause a backlash from the Sudanese government, which includes the enforce-ment of visa requirements for journalists wishing to enter the south.

In what is an effort likely to minimize the humiliation associated with the famine, the Khartoum government has instituted a practice of delay-ing or denying outright visas for journalists. The UN, in turn, not wishing to antagonize the government, has instituted a practice of not allowing journalists on relief flights without visas from the government. This leaves only NGO charters or charters paid for by the news organization. Miller described trying to cover Somalia: "We could fly into Mogadishu, or any one of the several cities in the south where the famine was, with relative ease. The UN took us in at no cost."[45] With so much to cover with limited time and resources, journalists go in the direction of least resistance. That does not describe the southern Sudan.

The practice of enforcing the visa requirement was instituted in late 1992, soon after a particularly hard-hitting CNN report on the war and drought upset Khartoum.[46] As a result, the UN agreed to the restrictions on undocumented reporters. As James Baker, a UN official, said in an interview, "It is a matter of sovereignty. We [the UN] have to respect that." Nor was he impressed by the argument that visa requirements actually stand in the way of journalists. "It is my experience," he remarked, "that if journalists want to cover something, they will find a way of doing it." [47]

Enforcing the visa requirement has also created tension, however subtle, between the press corps in Nairobi and OLS. "They're playing by the dictator's rules," reported Robert Press of the *Christian Science Monitor*. "As long as they require a visa to get on their planes, they're not going to get press coverage. It is as simple as that."[48] Lorch of the *New York Times* stated: "I don't have three months to wait for a visa."[49]

The government in Khartoum is not alone in its efforts to control travel in the South. Both factions of the SPLA require travel documents to enter rebel-controlled territory. With the right telephone call from the correct UN officials in Nairobi, however, obtaining these permits does not seem to present much of a problem. Both may be collected in forty-eight hours.

Safety

"Traditionally," noted the *New York Times*'s John Kifner, "when refugees are streaming out of some place, journalists are going in. But how to cover a war—and when to leave—is one of the most difficult problems in journalism. Miscalculations can be fatal."[50]

Somalia, of course, presented a particularly difficult challenge for the American press corps. In July 1993, four journalists were stoned to death by angry crowds, and in September, five Somali CNN employees were killed.[51] By October, there were no American television journalists reporting from Somalia. Instead, Somali freelancers obtained footage for American networks.[52]

Personal safety "was a problem in Central America. It's been a problem here."[53] Reid Miller spoke from experience, having been wounded covering the war in Nicaragua in 1984. His colleague, Terry Leonard, has in the past two years been posted to Bosnia, Somalia, and Nairobi; he was one of the first Western correspondents to make it into Rwanda during the civil war. For him, the danger "is just a part of life."

Though not as dangerous as Somalia in 1993, the southern Sudan presents its own unique blend of danger. As in any guerrilla war, the conflict lacks clear divisions. One is never sure where neutrality, if not safety, lies. In September 1992, a freelance journalist was killed in eastern Equatoria. He and a Burmese relief worker were shot in the back at close range. Rival factions of the SPLA blamed one another for the murders.[54] Also in 1992, an AID employee in Juba was apparently executed by Khartoum government authorities for treason.[55] Another AID employee was also killed at about the same time.

So in addition to logistical and legal barriers, safety concerns prevent closer coverage in the southern Sudan, as in any war-ravaged area.

News Attention Cycle

The long-simmering crisis in the Sudan has time and again been displaced by other more intense crises in the region. In the mid-1980s, it was Ethiopia. In 1990–91, it was Iraq and Kuwait. After the Gulf War, it was Somalia. Then as Somalia passed, news from Rwanda took over. In each instance, a more intense, concentrated crisis pushed aside any possibility of sustained attention to the Sudan. As Parmelee noted in an interview, "The world seems to have an appetite for only one crisis at a time." [56]

The problems associated with the public's limited attention horizon are made all the worse by its equally limited attention span. Downs called this phenomenon the "issue attention cycle"—"a systematic cycle of heightening public interest and then increasing boredom with major issues." Downs was interested in issue attention cycles regarding domestic problems, such as environmental issues.[57] But the same framework works just as well with foreign affairs. It is rooted, said Downs, "both in the nature of certain domestic problems and in the way major communications media interact with the public." Public attention to some issues, particularly distant ones which do not directly affect them, is invariably cyclical. Thus, as Bosso notes in his analysis of the Ethiopian famine, "a grave condition may exist long before public attention gets focused on it through some type of 'alarmed discovery.'"[58] What follows is "euphoric" public involvement in the search for a quick solution. As enthusiasm wanes, "the issue's apparent intractability remands the matter into a 'limbo' of low saliency and the reassertion of 'normal' politics. The issue may reemerge spasmodically, but it no longer is 'new.'"[59]

In the case of the Ethiopian famine in 1984, the trigger was BBC video footage that generated subsequent American network coverage. With the Sudan, there have not been any triggering devices. As mentioned earlier, attention paid to Somalia is partially explained by the fact that suffering was concentrated in a limited geographical area. When CNN gave greater attention to the Sudan in October 1992, the government began its practice of excluding journalists.

Besides the "victim dispersion problem," the war and famine in the Sudan do not offer the sharp dramatic qualities so evident in other crises of note in the region. Year in and year out the war has dragged on, as most news accounts written about it note. There is, to use the language of gatekeeping, nothing unique about it. Rather than a man-bites-dog story, it is a dog-bites-man nonstory. One State Department official noted: "Somalia evolved quickly. It was a sick patient who suddenly took a turn for the worse. Sudan is a terminal case that just keeps hanging on."

Somalia was also an extraordinary story, the first totally "failed" state. Nothing like it had been seen in modern history. As Richburg wrote, "Unlike other civil conflicts that have moved toward resolution with the end of the Cold War—in Angola, Cambodia, and El Salvador—the battle in Mogadishu involves no competing ideological issues and was not fueled by the U.S.- Soviet geopolitical rivalry." News accounts focused on the random, senseless violence, and on the utter chaos of Mogadishu and elsewhere in Somalia. A U.S. government official put it this way: "Somalia has ceased to exist."[60] The unique nature of the total collapse of civil society in Somalia was a different angle, especially when compared to the same old story out of the Sudan.

Opening Closed Gates

Since the end of the cold war, the explosion of interest in media coverage of humanitarian crises has produced several good analyses.[61]

Suggestions from this literature have included designating and training development journalists. They would, much as their counterparts in politics and finance beats, receive special training to assist them in preparing to write on development and disaster issues. Aid organizations should also train their personnel to work with the media, systematically evaluate media content, and conduct evaluations of communication strategies.

UN officials in Nairobi and representatives of the NGO community have attempted to evaluate their own communications strategies. With adjustment, their strategies may also be applied to other relief organization efforts in other parts of the world.

Further suggestions for OLS specifically (but applicable more generally) include the following:

— Although both OLS and the World Food Program (WFP) in Nairobi have dedicated and very capable information specialists, there is a serious need for trained, responsible UN and/or NGO press officers in places such as Lokichokio. If possible, a trained press officer should also accompany journalists while in the Sudan. The purpose would not be to lead journalists to only the "good story," but rather to address questions, serve as a source, or suggest alternative "takes" on a situation.

Press officers in the United States commonly serve as intermediaries between journalists and sources within an institution. They also serve as a sounding boards to journalists preparing a story. Although press officers in the Pentagon or the White House certainly cannot "kill" a pending story, it is common for journalists to call a spokesperson while working on a story to check facts. They may not answer necessarily all of the reporter's questions, but they will not lie; press officers lacking in credibility do not last long.

— Besides trained press officers, UN and NGO personnel should be given some media training. Most important, the relationship between public support for relief operations and news media coverage should be made clear.[62]

— The logistical difficulties are made greater by the legal ones. Until at least all of the Nairobi-based journalists have visas for the Sudan, not too much coverage can be expected.

— Communication facilities must be upgraded. A more reliable fax or teletype system should be put in place. Communication obstacles, however, will prove to be less of a burden as new satellite systems come on-line.

Notes

1. Pamela J. Shoemaker, *Communication Concepts 3: Gatekeeping* (Newbury Park, Calif., 1991).

2. Cost here refers to Anthony Downs's notion of information costs—the relative difficulty or ease experienced by the news consumer in gaining exposure to a news item. For example, as of this writing, relatively little cost, measured in time and effort, is required to learn the latest details of the O. J. Simpson trial. News of the trial seems nearly ubiquitous; information costs are therefore low. On the other hand, as the data presented later will suggest, news of the Sudan requires careful research using news archives, computer data banks, and monographs written by experts. There are, in short, high information costs involved in learning more about the Sudan.

3. Kurt Lewin, "Frontiers in Group Dynamics: II. Channels of Group Life; Social Planning and Action Research," *Human Relations* (1947), 143–53.

4. Ibid., 144.

5. Kurt Lewin, *Field Theory in Social Science: Selected Theoretical Papers* (New York, 1951), 187.

6. James. D. Halbran, Philip Elliott, and Graham Murdock, *Demonstrations and Communication: A Case Study* (Baltimore, 1970), 131.

7. Though space limitations do not allow for its development here, some scholars place greater emphasis on the political and ideological factors that come into play in news decision-making. Gates are not, in this view, simply naturally occurring phenomena, but rather are established and controlled by politically powerful actors (usually in government) and not by editors and reporters. For example, officials, as the dominant authoritative source in news stories, have an extraordinary ability to frame issues and events. As a result, the perceived relevance of events to the national interest is heavily influenced by elite framing, not the intrinsic qualities of the events. See W. Lance Bennett, *News: The Politics of Illusion* (New York, 1995); Jarol Manheim, *All of the People All of the Time: Strategic Communication and American Politics* (Armonk, N.Y., 1991); *The Evolution of Influence: Strategic Public Diplomacy and American Foreign Policy* (New York, 1994). Steven Livingston, *The Terrorism Spectacle* (Boulder, Colo., 1994).

8. Shoemaker, *Gatekeeping.*

9. Quoted in Don Oberdorfer, "The Path to Intervention; A Massive Tragedy 'We Could Do Something About,'" *Washington Post* (December 6, 1992), A1.

10. United States Committee on Refugees, *World Refugee Survey 1994* (Washington, D.C., 1995), 68.

11. Karl Maier, "Angola's War Burns On, And Thousands Starve; Battles in Central Region Cut Food Supplies," *Washington Post* (February 7, 1994), A12.

12. *World Refugee Survey 1994,* 70.

13. Jennifer Parmelee, "Sudan's Hidden Disaster; Africa's Longest War Leaves Millions at Risk," *Washington Post* (January 26, 1994), A1.

14. *World Refugee Survey 1994.*

15. Unpublished Operation LifeLine Sudan information packet.

16. United States Committee on Refugees, *Quantifying Genocide in Southern Sudan: 1983–1993* (Washington, D.C., 1993).

17. Jennifer Parmelee, "Out of Spotlight, Sudanese Crisis Said Arising; U.N. Says 1 Million Displaced Villagers At Risk as Civil War Obstructs Food, Medicine," *Washington Post* (September 15, 1992), A12.

18. Jennifer Parmelee, "Sudan's Hidden Disaster; Africa's Longest War Leaves Millions at Risk," *Washington Post* (January 26, 1994), A1.

19. See James F. Larson, *Television's Window on the World: International Affairs Coverage on the U.S. Networks* (Norwood, N.J., 1984); Roger Wallis and Stanley Baran, *The Known World of Broadcast News: International News and the Electronic Media* (London, 1990).

20. Interview, Washington, D.C., October 21, 1994.

21. However, with some changes in personnel, particularly in the *New York Times* bureau, this is not uniformly true. Also, not all coverage originates with the Nairobi bureaus. Jennifer Parmelee of the *Washington Post*, for example, works out of Addis Ababa, Ethiopia.

22. Blaine Harden, "From Our Far-Flung Correspondent: Out in the Bush, It Doesn't Hurt to Carry a Canteen—and a Spare Truck," *Washington Post* (September 21, 1986), C1.

23. Interview, Nairobi, Kenya, May 25, 1994.

24. Jennifer Parmelee, "Sudan's Hidden Disaster; Africa's Longest War Leaves Millions at Risk," *Washington Post* (January 26, 1994), A1.

25. Interview, Nairobi, Kenya, June 6, 1994.

26. Telephone interview, October 28, 1994.

27. Telephone interview, October 28, 1994.

28. Michael, Maren, "Feeding the Famine," *Forbes Media Critic* (Fall 1994), 30–38.

29. Interview with Reid Miller, Nairobi, Kenya, May 25, 1994.

30. Interview, Nairobi, Kenya, June 1, 1994.

31. Interview, Washington, D.C., October 27, 1994.

32. Interview, Washington, D.C., September 29, 1994.

33. Interview with Reid Miller, Nairobi, Kenya, May 25, 1994.

34. Interview, Nairobi, Kenya, May 23, 1994.

35. Interview with Donatella Lorch, of the *New York Times*, Nairobi, Kenya, May 23, 1994.

36. Keith B. Richburg, "African Press Endangered; Kenya, Others Pursue Journalists Despite Trend Toward Democracy," *Washington Post* (June 14, 1994), A1.

37. Pat Reber, "Kenyans Arrest Reporter's Wife," *Washington Post* (September 24, 1994), A19.

38. Alan Cowell, "Zimbabwe Imposes Press Curbs," *New York Times* (August 7, 1983), 14.

39. Alex Jones, "Pretoria's Press Curbs Limiting Coverage of Strife," *New York Times* (March 1, 1987), 20. See also Jarol Manheim and Robert B. Albritton, "Changing National Images: International Public Relations and Media Agenda Setting," *American Political Science Review*, 78 (1984), 641–54.

40. In June 1986, ABC News included coverage of South Africa in its evening news broadcast on twenty-six days, compared with six days in January 1987. CBS News evening news shows included coverage of South Africa on twenty-one days in

June and seven in January 1987. NBC News included South African news coverage on seventeen nights in June 1986, but only on three in January 1987.

41. Interview, Nairobi, Kenya, May 22, 1994.

42. Francis M. Deng and Larry Minear, *The Challenges of Famine Relief: Emergency Operations in the Sudan* (Washington, D.C., 1992).

43. Deng and Minear, *Challenges of Famine Relief*, 45.

44. Interview, Washington, D.C., October 21, 1994.

45. Interview with Reid Miller, Nairobi, Kenya, May 25, 1994.

46. Gary Strieker, "Famine in Sudan Persists Despite U.N. Relief Efforts," October 27, 1992. Transcript # 216–4.

47. Telephone interview with James Baker, November 8, 1994. Also interviewed on November 11, 1994, was Jan Eliasson, the former UN undersecretary-general for Humanitarian Affairs, now with the Swedish Foreign Ministry.

48. Interview, Nairobi, Kenya, June 6, 1994.

49. Interview with Donatella Lorch, Nairobi, Kenya, May 23, 1994.

50. John Kifner, "Reporters Stay a Long-Distance Call Away," *New York Times* (October 10, 1993), A3.

51. Donatella Lorch, "Safety Concerns Limit the Ability Of Reporters to Work in Somalia," *New York Times* (October 7, 1993), A11; Keith Richburg, "Somali Mob Kills Three Journalists," *Washington Post* (July 13, 1993), A1.

52. Howard Kurtz, "No American Journalists Reporting From the Scene," *Washington Post* (October 6, 1993), A13.

53. Interview with Reid Miller, Nairobi, Kenya, May 25, 1994.

54. Committee for the Protection of Journalists, *Attacks on the Press: A Comprehensive World Survey, 1992* (New York, 1993), 84.

55. Jane Perlez, "U.S. Is Appalled by the Execution of A.I.D. Employee in the Sudan," *New York Times* (September 23, 1992), A6.

56. Telephone interview, October 28, 1994.

57. Anthony Downs, *An Economic Theory of Democracy* (New York, 1957).

58. Christopher Bosso, "Setting the Agenda: Mass Media and the Discovery of Famine in Ethiopia," in Michael Margolis and Gary A. Mauser (eds.), *Manipulating Public Opinion: Essays on Public Opinion as a Dependent Variable* (Monterey, Calif., 1989), 155.

59. Ibid., 155.

60. Keith Richburg, "Peace Effort in Somalia Meets Initial Failure; One Feuding Side Rebuffs U.N. Mediation," *Washington Post* (January 4, 1992), A18.

61. Fred H. Cate (ed.), *International Disaster Communications: Harnessing the Power of Communications to Avert Disasters and Save Lives* (Washington, D.C., 1994), is certainly one of the best. Furthermore, his 1993 Washington Annenberg Program roundtable discussion, "Media, Disaster Relief, and Images of the Developing World: Strategies for Rapid, Accurate, and Effective Coverage of Complex Stories From Around the Globe," clearly sets forth several general strategies for accomplishing the goals articulated in the title. As general goals, these and the other suggestions offered by Cate are on target.

62. Open hostility toward the press was evident during my stay in camp. Without a trained press officer, one of the World Food Program (WFP) relief managers was

the first person journalists were brought to see by a stand-in press relations person. This manager, however, was working twelve- to sixteen-hour days, simply trying to get food and supplies to the refugees. He did not have time to drop everything to speak with reporters. On two occasions I witnessed journalists from Europe refused interviews. On deadline, they needed—or at least wanted—their interview with him immediately, within the hour of their arrival in camp. The manager, on the other hand, was trying to resolve a problem with the next day's shipment of relief supplies north. He therefore declined to be interviewed, and the journalists left.

His sentiments were summed up when he said, "They [journalists] come in here and demand to be paid attention to, demand for me to drop everything and give them their interview. It ain't gonna happen." In his view, the best journalists are "those who come in and spend a few days with us, see what we are about, eat and drink with us here. Instead, they come in here demanding instant attention." The nature of the job of a journalist, however, is in part defined by deadlines. Trained press officers in camp would be able to help journalists meet those deadlines while allowing people such as the WFP manager to get the relief supplies out. (David Richardson of the World Food Program, Lokichokio, Kenya, June 3, 1994.)

Although not a journalist, on a few occasions I also experienced open hostility from relief workers. For instance, one UN employee responsible for calculating the payload aboard planes forcefully pointed out to me that, because two journalists and I were on board the next day's flight, he would have to remove six bags of food. There seems to be a "those-of-us-on-the-front-lines" versus "those-on-the-outside" mind-set. This sense of mission is important for remaining motivated and committed in the midst of so much misery, but it also tends to put up walls against outsiders, such as journalists.

Part Two

BUILDING GREATER
HUMANITARIAN CAPACITY

CHAPTER FOUR

Big Problems, Small Print:
A Guide to the Complexity of
Humanitarian Emergencies and the Media

Peter Shiras

Introduction

IF HUMANITARIAN emergencies were ever simple, their complexity has grown enormously over the past five years. Even the jargon of relief professionals recognizes this reality. Man-made emergencies (typically a civil war combined with refugee flows), where natural factors may or may not be present, are now classified as "complex emergencies." Natural disasters, caused by floods, droughts, earthquakes, typhoons, and volcanic eruptions, are simple emergencies.

There is reality to the rhetoric. There have always been humanitarian emergencies caused by conflict (indeed, many natural phenomena only become emergencies because of man-made causes), but the prevalence of complex emergencies has been increasing since the end of the Cold War. Over the past several years, both the United Nations and the U.S. government's Office of Foreign Disaster Assistance (OFDA) have been responding primarily to complex rather than natural disasters. "Complexity" goes beyond the multiple factors that cause emergencies and extends to the international response apparatus seeking to provide relief and to the interplay of political, military, and relief institutions that seek to prevent and mitigate humanitarian emergencies.

The media have always been essential in shaping public opinion about and mobilizing public support for humanitarian crises. The role of television is particularly important in alerting the public to disasters, while the print media generally play a critical role in shaping attitudes toward the nature of a disaster. However, the U.S. media are largely unprepared for and structurally ill-suited to the task of conveying to their audience the complexity of distant problems of little apparent concern to Americans. Many relief officials and policy-makers also have too little understanding of the complex causes of humanitarian crises, of the international and national response structures, and of the dynamic nature of responses that can lead to effective (or ineffective) rehabilitation, development, and peace. In addition, both print and electronic media have cut back on overseas bureaus, particularly in the developing world.

The issue is one not of conveying complexity for its own sake, but rather of conveying an accurate, balanced, and understandable view of complex events. The media also need to find a balance between conveying sheer horror and the emotional reactions to them, and the political, social, economic, military, cultural, and relief/development issues underlying crises that are essential to effective responses and resolution. Television is probably more suited to the former task, print media to the latter.

This chapter outlines several central issues in complex emergencies and describes the national and international response structure for emergencies, an understanding of which is critical for the media as well as for policy-makers and relief officials. The final section makes recommendations about how the media and the relief community can work together to provide more informed and enlightened coverage of emergencies in developing countries.

Critical Issues in Complex Humanitarian Emergencies

New Realities in the Post–Cold War Era

In addition to the dramatic increase in the number and intensity of complex humanitarian emergencies since the end of the Cold War, three far-reaching and fundamental changes have altered the nature of humanitarian relief, the relief community's view of the world, and the world's perception of humanitarian relief. These changes are the increasing involvement of military forces, both national and multilateral; challenges by the relief community to the principle of sovereignty; and the centrality of humanitarian issues to the foreign policy debate in the United

States and elsewhere. These changes cut across almost every aspect of humanitarian response.

Not long ago, it would have been anathema to civilian relief practitioners to work alongside the military. Organizations choosing to cooperate with the military in the past, as in Vietnam, did so at considerable risk to their credibility as professionals. Some relief organizations continue to believe that any cooperation with the military compromises their essential humanitarian missions. Nonetheless, the military is increasingly providing or protecting humanitarian assistance. Relief organizations, either by choice or by necessity, end up cooperating with military forces.

The growing reliance on the military in humanitarian operations calls for an appraisal. Military roles have included 1) the provision of logistical assistance in natural disasters, such as during the typhoon in Bangladesh; 2) the provision of airlift and other logistical support in conflict situations, such as in Bosnia and, at an early stage, in Somalia; 3) the provision of peacekeeping forces under traditional rules of engagement, with the consent of the parties on the ground to facilitate humanitarian operations, as in Mozambique; 4) the direct provision of relief supplies to populations at risk, such as in northern Iraq; and 5) the use of military forces, without the consent of local authorities, to act as peace enforcers in a hostile environment to provide security for humanitarian operations and to carry out other activities such as disarmament of the warring factions, as in Somalia.

Although unanimity will perhaps never be achieved on the appropriate role for the military, the experience to date suggests certain guidelines. First, the use of military forces for humanitarian assistance should be considered only as a last resort. Second, the military should be guided by the same humanitarian principles as those used by the International Committee of the Red Cross. Third, the role of the military should be carefully defined to ensure that extraneous agendas are not introduced by military or political authorities into the humanitarian activities. Fourth, the military should avoid engaging in any activities that can be effectively managed by civilians. The military should not have a residual role in humanitarian operations but rather should be called upon when civilian capacities are outstripped by the size, urgency, or insecurity of an emergency.

The military has generally performed with professionalism, but also at a very high financial cost. In Somalia, $10 was spent on military operations for every $1 spent on humanitarian programs. In addition, intended or not, the presence of a large military force, and the political decisions about how to use that force, can easily overwhelm, distort, and work at cross purposes to the achievement of humanitarian objectives.[1] Clear objectives, including a distinction between humanitarian and nation-building objectives, are essential for successful deployment of the military in humanitarian operations.

Second, through both word and deed, the relief community has contributed to a growing body of doctrine and precedent challenging the notion that intervention in the internal affairs of a state violates international law when it is carried out to save lives of those put at risk by the action or inaction of a host government.[2] Non-governmental organizations (NGOs) have been working on the basis of this principle for years and have received support from governments when it was in their political interests to ignore the claims to sovereignty of an offending regime. However, the UN system, too, is witnessing serious cracks in the sovereignty wall. Both the last secretary general and the current one have spoken of sovereignty as being less than absolute. While the international community continues to justify a resort to humanitarian intervention in terms of threats posed to "international peace and security," often the motivation to intervene comes primarily from the need to save lives.

Third, while humanitarian relief has sporadically arisen as an important political issue in the past (such as the use of so-called humanitarian assistance to the Nicaraguan *contras* during the Central American conflict), it has not traditionally occupied a central role as an instrument of U.S. foreign policy or as an element of international diplomacy. From Operation Provide Comfort in northern Iraq, through Operation Restore Hope in Somalia, to actions in Rwanda and Bosnia, humanitarian assistance has recently become a critical element in foreign policy debate both in this country and abroad. The consequences are by no means entirely salutary.

Many argue that relief aid has been used to avoid taking more substantive political or military actions in Bosnia. In other cases, military and political actions have been taken to provide humanitarian assistance, as in Somalia. As a result of the enormous levels of funding, the prevention of crises has now become one of the centerpieces of U.S. foreign policy. According to Brian Atwood, administrator of the United States Agency for International Development, "The Clinton administration has made crisis prevention a central theme of its foreign policy. The UN secretary general has embraced the need for preventive diplomacy."[3] As a result, the relief community finds itself at the center of a major foreign policy debate. It is often looked to for answers to questions about which it has a great deal of experience, but not a great deal of sophistication in translating operational expertise into policy prescription.

The sea change over a relatively short period of time regarding the role of the military, the limits of sovereignty, and the centrality of relief in the foreign policy debate provides the overall context, but it does not provide specific insights into a particular crisis. These dramatic changes have, however, contributed to confusion within the humanitarian relief community about the multiple causal factors, institutional actors, and operational challenges in complex emergencies. It is in these three areas that both media and relief practitioners face the greatest challenges to understand the role of their respective professions.

Causes of Conflict and Humanitarian Emergencies

While the causes of conflict and humanitarian emergencies are varied and usually related, both the media and humanitarian organizations are notorious for reducing complex causes to oversimplified and misleading slogans. The cause of conflict in Somalia becomes simply chaos, the fighting in Rwanda is reduced to ethnic violence, and the famine in Ethiopia in 1984–85 is viewed as a product simply of drought. There are elements of truth to all of these categorizations, but the underlying causes of conflict must be portrayed more accurately if both the public and policy-makers are to act wisely.

Both humanitarian organizations and the media have an interest in conveying a view of complex, distant problems in an oversimplified manner. Television news has very limited space for foreign news stories and tends to simplify complex problems for viewers who have probably never heard of Rwanda or Somalia. Much the same is true of local media, both print and electronic. National print media devote more space to foreign news stories and tend to reach more of an elite readership, thereby shaping the opinions of policy-makers.

Humanitarian organizations are often primarily interested in promoting a view of an emergency that is conducive to generating public sympathy and donations, but not necessarily reflecting complex realities. One of the points of guidance that the OFDA gives to its field workers in working with the media is, "Keep it simple. Simplify and summarize your major points. . . . Remember that the audience is the general public."[4]

To inform the general public more accurately, to contribute to better policy-making by governmental and multilateral authorities, and to improve the quality of relief efforts, both the relief community and the media need a fuller understanding of the causes of humanitarian emergencies. The cases of Somalia and Rwanda are instructive.

First, Somalia was awash in weapons, supplied by both the former Soviet Union and the United States during alternate periods of support of the Siad Barre regime by both superpowers. Developing countries' expenditures on arms rose from 7 percent of the world total in 1960 to 15 percent in 1987, with two-thirds of that spending outside of the Middle East in some of the poorest countries in the world.[5] Through both aid and trade, arms transfers to developing countries have not only taken resources away from human development but have also fueled internal conflicts. Arms transfers to Rwanda were a critical factor in its bloody civil war.[6]

Second, external support for repressive regimes has undergirded their often shaky hold on power and led to the continuation of regimes through repression, not consent. Once the Cold War ended and Somalia lost strategic value to the United States, President Barre's days were numbered. His divide-and-rule tactics had set one clan against another. This dynamic largely eluded the public portrayal of clan violence by divorcing it from its historical context. It is no coincidence that Liberia, Zaire, the Sudan, and Somalia, all countries mired in conflict, were major recipients during the Cold War of U.S. foreign aid because they supported its geopolitical objectives, even though they were highly repressive.

In the case of Rwanda, the French, and to a lesser extent the Belgians, were the main external supporters of a regime that became increasingly dictatorial over time. French support did not halt with the end of the Cold War, and the French repeatedly stepped in to save President Habyarimana's regime when it was threatened. This political strategy ultimately proved unsustainable, with tragic consequences for the Rwandan people.

Third, regardless of outside support, repressive, authoritarian regimes create conflict and humanitarian crises. While that may seem self-evident, it is a point often neglected in both media coverage and in humanitarian relief and recovery programs. One of the most effective preventive strategies for avoiding humanitarian emergencies is the existence of a free press, as well as freedom of movement and association. Through a free press, impending crises may be identified and pressure brought to bear upon governments to take preventive action. Where these conditions do not exist, problems quickly turn into emergencies.

Fourth, struggles over scarce resources are also accentuating conflict. A recent analysis of internal conflict gave prominence to competition over natural resources. "Rapid population growth and environmental degradation are also continuing threats that tempt potentially dangerous conflicts in several regions. Disputes over the Middle East's scarce water could worsen and Africa's chronic poverty, low agricultural production, and environmental deterioration persist as the breeding grounds for violence."[7] In Rwanda, resource constraints also contributed to conflict, but, as one commentator has stated, "The present conflicts are largely the result of a competition between elites for the benefits of public power. . . . High population densities, or high population growth rates. . . . do not automatically bring about environmental degradation or famine. The quality of government policies is a more important determinant."[8]

As the economic and human cost of emergencies grows, policy-makers are focusing increasingly on prevention to head off crises. Preventive diplomacy is now a cornerstone of the UN's Agenda for Peace, and crisis prevention is central to U.S. foreign policy. NGOs traditionally involved in relief now find themselves forced to consider conflict prevention strategies.

The media played a key role in drawing attention to Somalia once it was a major humanitarian crisis, but media coverage of Somalia was limited before then. In contrast, media coverage of Rwanda during the period of genocide was extensive but provoked no large-scale international response until refugee flows began. Galvanizing early action remains one of the central challenges to the international community. The lack of political will to act early enough in response to conflicts and the inadequacy of preventive diplomacy and peace-building have been central failures.

This review of causal factors is far from exhaustive and is intended to suggest the interrelatedness of causal factors in conflict and humanitarian emergencies. Causal factors are both external and internal to the affected country, and they result largely from policy choices that can be influenced by governments, as well as by relief and development practitioners. This review also highlights areas often neglected by the media in their coverage and by humanitarian practitioners in their understanding of crises.

The National and International Humanitarian Response System

Describing the various institutional actors who respond to humanitarian emergencies and their interactions as a "system" may stretch credulity.

However, there are well-established players and patterns in the response to emergencies. An understanding of who they are and what they do is crucial to the media seeking to gather and communicate information and to humanitarian practitioners seeking to improve humanitarian response mechanisms.

Most analyses of the humanitarian relief system focus on international responses to emergencies and neglect the national and indigenous institutions that are often central. One of the most serious weaknesses of both media reporting on emergencies and humanitarian relief programs is the failure to consult indigenous organizations.[9] The failure to incorporate indigenous knowledge and organizations into international relief efforts undermines both their effectiveness and the transition to recovery.

Six primary types of institutions respond to emergencies, with subsets within each type. Each of these types of institutions has certain strengths and weaknesses and certain interests and perspectives on humanitarian response.[10]

The United Nations System

The United Nations system relates to humanitarian emergencies on at least three different levels, much the way many governments do: humanitarian, political, and military. The synthesis of these different relationships, to the extent that it occurs, takes place in the office of the secretary general or through the special representatives of the secretary general.

The UN system consists of three primary humanitarian operational agencies: the United Nations Children's Fund (UNICEF), the UN High Commission for Refugees (UNHCR), and the World Food Program (WFP). The Department of Humanitarian Affairs (DHA) was established in 1991 both to coordinate the operational humanitarian work of the UN system and to engage in "humanitarian diplomacy." The specialized UN organizations operate with a high degree of autonomy, and the under secretary general for humanitarian affairs attempts to coordinate by persuasion but without any effective statutory authority.

The roles of UNHCR with refugees, UNICEF with children, and WFP with food are usually the highest profile UN programs. Because of their particular mandates, however, there often are overlaps and gaps in their coverage. UNHCR works with refugees but may or may not work with internally displaced persons. All UN agencies have difficulty working in areas outside of government control because they are inter-governmental organizations, although UNICEF is often more flexible in this regard.

Other UN agencies may also be involved in the operational side of humanitarian emergencies. The United Nations Development Program (UNDP) has the role of being the lead UN agency in countries, and the resident representative of UNDP serves as the emergency coordinator unless and until the secretary general or DHA designates an alternative. The Food and Agriculture Organization gets involved primarily in crop assessments that play a role in early warning of impending emergencies. Recently, the high commissioner for human rights and the Human Rights Center have been involved in the deployment of human rights monitors in Rwanda and other emergencies.

The Department of Political Affairs (DPA) plays the lead role within the UN system in the political dimensions of humanitarian emergencies. DHA's role in humanitarian diplomacy and DPA's role in political nego-tiations may overlap, but the former is intended to engage specifically in humanitarian issues (such as humanitarian access) while the latter seeks to address the overall framework for peace.

The Department of Peace-Keeping Operations is responsible for the deployment of blue helmets under Chapter VI authority, implying consent of the local authorities, light arms for troops, and a traditional peace-keeping mandate. These troops may also fall under Chapter VII authority, which does not require consent of the concerned government, involves heavy armament, and implies peace enforcement.

The UN has been a convenient scapegoat for failed missions, which are as much the result of a lack of political will by member states and, particularly, the United States. Washington blocked early UN efforts to become involved in Somalia in 1992. The "mission creep" in Somalia was approved by all the Security Council's members. The eighteen U.S. soldiers killed in Mogadishu in October 1993 were under direct U.S., not UN, command.

Nonetheless, UN relief operations often suffer from dysfunctional bureaucratic structures and regulations. The lack of coordination among UN agencies has not been effectively resolved through the creation of DHA. Responsiveness to emergencies has been hampered by security regulations, although these, too, are changing. Early UN diplomatic efforts in Somalia were ill-informed and counterproductive.

Donor Governments

Donor governments replicate the UN system in the involvement of humanitarian, political, and military dimensions in their response to emergencies. The U.S. government is the most relevant example of the complexity and comprehensiveness of emergency response.

On the humanitarian side, the OFDA, within the Agency for International Development, is the official response agency. OFDA is located within the Bureau of Humanitarian Response, which also houses the Food For Peace Office (FFP). FFP is responsible for providing food aid in emergency situations. A new Office of Transition Initiatives was created in 1993 to meet the needs of transitional periods in countries moving from complex emergencies to peace. Such initiatives include demining, demobilization, reintegration of ex-soldiers, and other activities not adequately covered by either emergency or development programs. At the same time, the Bureau of Refugee Programs within the State Department has responsibility for responding to worldwide refugee problems.

At the political level, both the National Security Council (NSC) and the State Department play an active role in the political dimensions of humanitarian emergencies, and both have established offices to deal specifically with humanitarian matters. The NSC now has an office for Global Issues, within which is a division handling humanitarian affairs. Likewise, the State Department has created an Office of Global Affairs, which includes responsibility for refugees and humanitarian crises.

The Department of Defense (DOD) is involved in humanitarian emergencies both through the direct involvement of U.S. troops, when called upon by the president, and through an Office of Refugee and Humanitarian Affairs. The expanded DOD role in humanitarian affairs dates to 1986, although in the past several years DOD's involvement has accelerated. As a result of its more intensive involvement in humanitarian operations, the Pentagon is now developing operational guidance for its troops in the field.[11] U.S. military forces may be activated on a unilateral basis (Bangladesh), as part of a U.S.-led multilateral force sanctioned by the UN (Haiti), or as part of a UN peacekeeping operation (UNOSOM II in Somalia.)

Washington's response to complex emergencies has been curtailed because of new policies regarding peacekeeping, concerns about costs, the reaction to the death of American soldiers in Mogadishu, and insufficient attention to preventive measures. PPD25, a presidential policy document, outlines very restrictive conditions under which the United States would either commit its own troops to peacekeeping missions or support peacekeeping in the United Nations. Concerns about the spiraling cost of peacekeeping have further dampened support for peacekeeping. The "Somalia syndrome," a reaction to the loss of American lives in Mogadishu, has soured both the executive and the legislative branches of government on humanitarian intervention.[12] Finally, dwindling resources for development assistance to attack the root causes of conflict and the low priority of preventive diplomacy contribute to a crisis in U.S. leadership regarding humanitarian responses.

The International NGO Community

International NGOs are one of the four pillars of the international relief system, but they are a diverse lot with their own set of strengths and weaknesses. NGOs are often credited with being flexible, quick to respond, unburdened by bureaucratic constraints, in touch with local realities, and highly committed to the task at hand. At the same time, many demonstrate uneven degrees of professionalism, tend to work on a small scale, often ignore the political and military context in which they work, and resist coordination.

International NGOs may be divided into at least three organizational types: relief, relief and development, and advocacy. All three are involved in humanitarian emergencies in different ways. Relief organizations limit their involvement to the emergency phase and tend not to focus on issues of long-term recovery. They also tend to bring sectoral expertise to emergency work. Relief and development organizations tend to have less sectoral expertise in emergencies but may have a longer history in a given country working on development before and after an emergency. Advocacy organizations are usually focused on an issue (refugees or human rights, for example) or an area. Advocacy groups tend to have a great deal of expertise in both the issues of concern to them and the geographical area of involvement, but they may lack an appreciation of the operational environment in which humanitarian practitioners are working.

A growing trend within the NGO community is the extension of their work from the humanitarian to the political level in attempting to influence military, diplomatic, and humanitarian policy. Many relief and development organizations are increasing their advocacy as they recognize the crucial role that policy plays in the lives of those they are attempting to assist and in the success or failure of their own programs. An increasing number of NGOs are also looking more seriously at the issue of conflict resolution as it affects their relief and development programs. In this way, NGOs are recognizing the importance of the political sphere for their relief activities while trying to preserve the impartiality and nonpartisan nature of their humanitarian work. NGOs face at least two major challenges in the operational side of their work: to professionalize further their work and avoid contributing to conflict through inadvertent actions.

In response to a humanitarian emergency, relief practitioners are expected to be able to fulfill a vast array of tasks: to act immediately to save lives; to understand and respect the local culture; to consult with and incorporate indigenous groups into relief operations; to identify needs and secure resources to meet them; to overcome logistical difficulties; to negotiate safe passage with governmental, military, and rebel forces; to live in unhealthy and unsafe conditions; to maintain emotional balance; to keep records of all finances; to account for all food and other commodities; to manage their staffs; to inform their headquarters with status reports; and, not least, to speak to the press. Relief practitioners face overwhelming obligations, some of which are inconsistent one with another and all of which require high degrees of professionalism.

As the number of emergencies worldwide grows and the entire relief system is stretched to the breaking point, the need for greater specialization and professionalism is self-evident. Those organizations with sectoral expertise are among the most effective, but technical expertise is only one of the many areas in which NGOs require greater professionalization. One of the priority needs that InterAction, a coalition of U.S.-based NGOs, has identified among its members is training in specialized areas of emergency operations.

Equally important is the need to understand humanitarian law and principles; to know the local political, economic, and social reality; to have strong negotiating skills; to be able to manage staff effectively in highly unstable situations; and to have strong accountability systems in place. Given that most emergency situations are dangerous, it is a testimony to the commitment of relief workers that the system works as well as it does. Commitment, however important, must be combined with greater professionalism if the challenges of responding to emergencies are to be met.

Ironically, one of the central dilemmas of relief work in armed conflict is that if it is not properly managed, it can do more harm than good by exacerbating the conflict that gives rise to the humanitarian crisis in the first place. Often relief workers strive to do no harm, but they are forced to balance the good that they do against the harm. The negative consequences of relief operations were clearly visible in Somalia, when large amounts of food were being looted by clan militias and sold on the commercial market to finance the warlord effort. In Rwanda, the dilemma is most clearly manifested in the control which Hutu military forces exert over the refugee camps in Zaire, diverting food supplies, threatening relief workers, and intimidating those considering repatriation.[13]

Beyond the need to avoid fueling a conflict through relief programs, relief practitioners are also looking at ways in which relief programs can be used to foster reconciliation. By bringing antagonists together with a common humanitarian objective, humanitarian operations can be used to build bridges between belligerents. For example, relief operations have been used in Liberia as a platform for conducting reconciliation workshops that explored the deeper roots of ethnic conflict in that country.

The converse, however, is also possible, in that the introduction of resources into a resource-scarce environment can exacerbate conflict. Without adequate accountability for food aid in Somalia, for example, much of the aid was diverted to support the war. When food aid was strictly accounted for, however, and cut off when it was abused, the adverse effect of diversion of resources was prevented. Thus, the challenge to the relief community is to look for ways that relief, without compromising the basic principles of impartiality, neutrality, and independence, can be used to foster a process of reconciliation or, at the very least, not exacerbate conflict.

The International Committee of the Red Cross

The ICRC is unique in that it has a very specific mandate spelled out by the Geneva Conventions on international humanitarian law. The ICRC provides relief to victims of conflict, particularly when those victims cannot be reached by any other organizations, and it also acts as the guardian and promoter of international humanitarian law. As such, it operates with the consent of both governments and rebel forces and abides by strict standards of neutrality and impartiality. Historically, the ICRC was staffed only by Swiss nationals, but the plethora of humanitarian emergencies has forced it to expand its recruitment to other nationalities. Most of its international staff, however, tend to be European.

The ICRC is distinct from but related to national Red Cross or Red Crescent societies grouped together under the International Federation of Red Cross and Red Crescent Societies. National societies are chartered by their respective governments and, while they are expected to abide by Red Cross principles, they often lack the independence that the ICRC guards so zealously. The ICRC is in principle opposed to the involvement of military forces in humanitarian programs because they undermine respect for international humanitarian law, which requires all belligerents to protect civilians and grant access for relief.

Host Country Governments and Authorities

The host country government or another political authority (for example, rebel forces) is important in relief efforts. In some countries, the host government has had a great deal of experience with emergencies and has a well-developed response structure. The Relief and Rehabilitation Commission in Ethiopia is one such example. This type of entity is responsible for donor coordination and implementation of relief programs at a governmental level. In most countries, however, such an entity either does not exist, is fairly ineffective, or is so highly politicized as to be counterproductive.

In addition to humanitarian response, the host government also plays important political and military roles. Indeed, it is usually the political and military policies of governmental and irregular authorities that have given rise to the humanitarian crisis. Often the creation of a humanitarian emergency is not just an unfortunate by-product of fighting between antagonists but rather is a deliberate strategy by one side or both to target the civilian population in the conflict.

Rebel forces have become increasingly sophisticated in setting up their own humanitarian relief operations, particularly when they control a sizable portion of territory. Usually they do this under the guise of an NGO in order to attract support from external donors. The Relief Society of Tigray, the Eritrean Relief Association, and the Sudan Relief and Rehabilitation Agency are all examples of such NGOs. Such agencies have been able to attract support from NGOs and governments in carrying out their relief activities and in some instances have operated with high degrees of professionalism. In other cases, they serve largely as fronts for the military forces and as channels of assistance to the military effort.

The Indigenous NGO Community

Indigenous NGOs, like international NGOs, are diverse. Indigenous NGOs vary tremendously in their independence from governmental or rebel authority, in the size and sophistication of their operations, and in their approach to relief and recovery programs. In addition to NGOs created by rebel forces, whose allegiances are transparent, many NGOs are either created by governments or have strong allegiances to governments. In repressive environments, which are the norm in conflict-ridden countries, indigenous NGOs may have very little political space, which makes independence from governments problematic.

Many NGOs, however, are truly independent from governmental authorities and provide critical links to communities for international organizations. All too often these local organizations are overlooked in the rush of donors to reach the needy. Indigenous NGOs offer the best partners for international organizations in making relief programs effective and in building up an indigenous capacity to respond to emergencies. While many local NGOs may start out small in size and initially have little professional capacity, these organizations may become large and highly accomplished if one of the goals of their international partners is to help them build that capacity.

Indigenous NGOs also vary tremendously in their approach to communities. Some NGOs have a fairly traditional approach motivated by charity, and they focus on commodity distribution. Other NGOs see relief programs as antithetical to development programs, as the distribution of relief may create dependency and undermine the motivation for self-sufficiency and community empowerment. Many indigenous NGOs fall somewhere between these two extremes.

As indigenous NGOs grow as implementers of and advocates for humanitarian relief programs, their importance to the media and international humanitarian organizations increases proportionately. In terms of an understanding of the cultural, political, social, economic, religious, and ethnic dimensions of conflicts, they are potentially some of the best interpreters of the local reality.

What conclusions should be drawn from this vast array of institutional actors involved in humanitarian responses? First, reconciling the interests of military, political, and humanitarian actors has proven the most difficult of objectives to achieve. Each set of actors has its own interests at stake, even if all are engaged in what would appear a common mission.

Humanitarian organizations will attempt to be neutral, while political interests will seek to identify which faction is worthy of support. The military is concerned first of all with security, both its own and that of the environment, which may or may not be consistent with long- and short-term political and humanitarian objectives. Both the media and humanitarian practitioners need to understand these dynamics more fully.

Second, while the need for coordination in emergency situations is axiomatic given scarce resources and numerous actors, the difficulty in coordinating among humanitarian organizations—let alone among humanitarian, political, and military elements—grows with the number and type of institutional actors. Coordination among humanitarian NGOs is a formidable challenge, and very much the same may be said for the different UN agencies. Some institutionalized coordination mechanisms have recently been established through the United Nations (DHA's coordinating role), the military (Civilian Military Operations Center), Humanitarian Assistance Centers, and OFDA (Disaster Assistance Response Teams). On the other hand, some governments seek to control humanitarian relief programs, particularly those of indigenous NGOs, under the guise of coordination.

Within the NGO community, several mechanisms exist to promote coordination among NGOs at the international and local levels. InterAction plays a very active role in coordination both among U.S.-based NGOs and with the UN and the U.S. government. The International Council of Voluntary Agencies (ICVA) has recently begun to play an active coordination role at the local level by establishing an NGO coordinating office in Rwanda. The Steering Committee for Humanitarian Response, ICVA, and InterAction all facilitate coordination between NGOs and the United Nations.

Finally, understanding the strengths and weaknesses of each type of institution in humanitarian responses is critical for both an effective program and media coverage. Expecting the military to airlift relief supplies to inaccessible areas uses its comparative advantage well, but asking the military to run a feeding program does not. Similarly, asking human rights monitoring organizations to assess the effectiveness of food delivery systems in a famine is not reflective of their areas of expertise, in contrast to asking them to analyze the human rights issues that undoubtedly are behind the reasons for the famine. Just as there is a great need for specialization and professionalism in what each operational agency does in an emergency, it is also important that the media understand the areas of professional expertise of their sources in relief organizations.

Recommendations

Two distinct but related issues need to be considered by both the media and humanitarian organizations. One is the view of the developing world that they portray and the extent to which it is balanced or skewed toward sensational images. The second is the accuracy and overall quality of information provided to and communicated by the media. The first issue requires an analysis of media coverage generally and, on the part of humanitarian organizations, requires an analysis of their fundraising, development education, and overall media strategy. Such an analysis goes beyond the scope of this paper.

The second issue, however, fits squarely into the preceding discussion focusing on the capacity of both the media and humanitarian organizations to understand and convey the complexity of emergencies. Given the media's critical role in mobilizing public support and influencing public policy, they are both observers of and participants in relief operations. The way that they convey the news about relief operations can do enormous good or serious damage, thus making the stakes of conveying a balanced, accurate, and comprehensive picture that much greater than it might be in other types of news coverage. Journalists often see themselves as simply reporting the facts as they see them. Yet the facts and images that they choose to cover influence the extent of external support for an emergency. In this way, journalists, wittingly or not, become participants in humanitarian operations simply by the way that they cover a story.

Recommendations for the media and humanitarian organizations should take into account the convergences in their respective interests and needs. Aid workers and journalists are often thrown together in unfamiliar environments far from their homes and will naturally be drawn to what is familiar, each other. Aid workers want coverage and journalists want sources. If neither speaks the local language, this, too, brings them together. Both journalists and aid workers tend to come in two varieties: young idealists who want to change the world and seasoned veterans who have seen it all and whose cynicism is reinforced by manifest human misery. Aid workers have logistical resources, and journalists need ways to move around.

Both the media and aid organizations have interests that are often at odds with portraying an accurate picture of emergencies. Relief organizations want publicity to help them with fundraising or to increase their influence. Therefore, they have an interest in dramatizing the desperate nature of and needs involved in a situation and care most about whether their organization's name is mentioned. Journalists want their stories to air or appear in print. Therefore, the more sensational the story, the greater its chances for publication.

Even so, the media's positive role in publicizing crises overseas is essential to effective international response. For all of the criticism, the importance of the media's role and its positive effect on mobilizing an international response to crises should not go unrecognized. Television images from Ethiopia in 1984 mobilized an unprecedented worldwide relief effort, notwithstanding the delay after relief agencies had sounded the alarm. Furthermore, criticism of the media's extensive portrayal of negative images is not limited to news from the developing world. Growing press criticism and cynicism in the United States by both media analysts and journalists themselves focus primarily on local and national news coverage.[14]

Another important, and often overlooked, dimension to the media and humanitarian emergencies is the role of local media. The recent experience in Rwanda and Burundi highlights the critical role of local media in conflict situations. In Rwanda, state radio broadcasters exhorted listeners to take up arms against the Tutsi minority and thereby encouraged the genocide that followed. In contrast, in Burundi the clergy of different religious denominations used the radio to send a message of calm and reconciliation to the population. In both cases, the power of the local media, in this case the radio, was of critical importance.

What can begin to overcome some of the inherent biases and interests that frustrate accurate and comprehensive news coverage of humanitarian emergencies?

Develop an Emergency Field Guide for the Media

All relief organizations have emergency field operational manuals that provide the technical resources to design and implement programs. The development of such a guide for the media would provide reporters, particularly those covering humanitarian crises for the first time; essential information about relief operations, including international and national relief systems; coordination mechanisms; basic information likely to be useful in all emergencies; the basics of international humanitarian law; and a synopsis of key operational principles that guide relief operations. InterAction has developed media guides for specific countries describing NGO activities and press contacts, but no user-friendly guide for the media exists that is equivalent to a field operations manual.

Such a guide would not be specific to any particular emergency but rather would be a user-friendly guide to the issues and actors in emergency situations. It could include a listing of major NGOs and UN and governmental organizations, their areas of expertise, and resource persons to contact. In addition, it could include a description of international humanitarian law, ICRC principles, and key issues for relief practitioners. It could also provide some basic information on emergencies as a reference for journalists.

Promote Professional Exchange between Journalists and Relief Workers

Relief workers should understand better the possibilities and constraints of working with the media, while journalists need to understand better the nature of the relief organizations. Such exchanges could be formal or informal, but the requirement for greater professional dialogue between the two communities outside the reporter/source relationship is apparent. Relief workers can learn to understand the approaches that appeal to journalists and how best to present new angles on stories. The media can learn more about the issues and constraints that relief professionals confront daily.

Broaden the Boundaries of Traditional Coverage

To project a different view of humanitarian crises than is generally portrayed, the media should broaden the boundaries of what is typically considered as news. Editors need to encourage foreign correspondents to analyze events behind the dramatic headlines and scrutinize other issues in emergencies, particularly the positive aspects of a country's own response to a crisis and the challenges and dilemmas that humanitarian crises pose for outsiders. Television coverage should not only focus on the dramatic needs in emergencies, but also cover recovery programs and emergencies which are averted.

While the idea of public or civic journalism is still being refined, the editors who are using this concept say that "instead of emphasizing conflict, they want news coverage to spur people to find solutions to political and community problems."[15] Such an approach could be usefully applied to conflict situations abroad wherein reporting would focus not only on the conflict, but also on an array of both indigenous and international strategies for dealing with the conflict. It could also apply to incipient crises before they become full-blown emergencies.

Develop a Comprehensive Media Strategy

Humanitarian organizations require a comprehensive media strategy in order to define exactly what messages they want to communicate. Most NGOs should have at least three separate objectives in using the media: fundraising, education of the general public, and policy influence. By explicitly articulating these objectives, humanitarian organizations could provide better guidance to their staff on how to interact with the media. Most operational organizations tend to think primarily about fund-raising in their contacts with the media, and this orientation supports a bias that may be antithetical to other organizational objectives of development education and advocacy.

Know Your Sources and Their Areas of Expertise

Relief organizations come in all sizes and shapes, and the responsible ones limit their comments to the press to the areas that they know best. Just as aid officials speaking off the record are obliged to know the reliability of the journalists to whom they are speaking, journalists need to know when an opinion is just that and when it is well grounded in expertise. This is not to suggest that only the people considered experts should be consulted, but rather that sources should be consulted in areas where they have demonstrated experience.

This issue is particularly problematic for journalists who parachute into an area with no background on the nature of the conflict and stay for very short periods of time. As news organizations have cut back on overseas bureaus, particularly in Africa, this is a serious and growing problem.

Promote, and Cover Indigenous Expertise and Programs

Both relief organizations and reporters tend to overlook indigenous sources of experience. Reporting on humanitarian crises can provide a more balanced picture of indigenous self-help by highlighting the programs of local organizations in a manner reflective of their actual involvement. International aid officials can promote such reporting by facilitating contact between their indigenous partner organizations and journalists. An important corollary to reporting on indigenous programs is the role that the local media play in mitigating or inflaming a conflict. The international media and humanitarian organizations should promote local professionalism. This goal should also be a major objective of programs seeking to build democratic institutions abroad with a focus on supporting a free, responsible, and professional press.

Notes

1. Peter Shiras, "The Lessons of Somalia," *Monday Developments* (April 11, 1994), 9.

2. Catholic Relief Services, "Guidelines for Humanitarian Assistance in Conflict Situations," April 1992; Larry Minear and Thomas G. Weiss, *Humanitarian Action in Times of War* (Boulder, Colo., 1993).

3. Brian Atwood, "Suddenly, Chaos," *Washington Post* (July 31, 1994).

4. Office of Foreign Disaster Assistance, USAID, *Field Operations Guide for Disaster Assessment and Response* (Washington, D.C., 1994), I-4.

5. United Nations Development Program, *Human Development Report 1994* (New York, 1994), 49–50.

6. Human Rights Watch, *Arming Rwanda: The Arms Trade and Human Rights Abuses in the Rwandan War* (New York, 1994).

7. Michael S. Lund, "Preventive Diplomacy and American Foreign Policy: A Guide for the Post-Cold War Era" (Washington, D.C., 1994), 37.

8. Peter Uvin, "Don't Blame Tribal Hatred for Conflict in Burundi and Rwanda," *George St. Journal* (Providence, R.I., 1994), 4.

9. Fred H. Cate, *Media, Disaster Relief and Images of the Developing World* (Washington, 1994).

10. For a lengthy discussion of these actors, see Larry Minear and Thomas G. Weiss, *Mercy Under Fire: War and the Global Humanitarian Community* (Boulder, Colo., 1995).

11. Air Land Sea Application Center, "Multi-Service Procedures for Humanitarian Assistance Operations" (March 1994).

12. See Thomas G. Weiss, "Overcoming the Somalia Syndrome—'Operation Restore Hope'?" *Global Governance*, 1 (May-August 1995), 171–87.

13. Raymond Bonner, "Rwandans Who Massacred Now Terrorizing Camps," *New York Times* (October 31, 1994), 1.

14. William Glaberson, "The New Press Criticism: News as the Enemy of Hope," *New York Times* (October 9, 1994), D1.

15. William Glaberson, "A New Press Role: Solving Problems," *New York Times* (October 3, 1994), D6.

CHAPTER FIVE

Emergency Response as Morality Play:
The Media, the Relief Agencies, and the Need for Capacity Building

John C. Hammock and Joel R. Charny

BY NOW the television images are all too familiar: the North American or English foreign correspondent, in multipocketed vest, describing the grim scene, with teeming masses of suffering Africans or Asians in the background; the Irish nurse giving the tour of the emergency ward or feeding center; the children, strangely lifeless, staring soundlessly into the camera; the soldiers from the evil regime or the ragtag guerrillas menacing people with the power that comes from the guns they wield. These are among the images that have come to define international humanitarian emergencies to the public.

These images are at once backdrop and centerpiece of what has become over the years a scripted morality play. The crisis arrives with the suddenness and power of an earthquake. Then, the international community—a mix of United Nations agencies, the Red Cross, private relief organizations, and, increasingly, the militaries of the industrialized countries or the developing world (the latter almost always under UN auspices)—responds as rapidly as possible to the emergency.

Initially, the response is heroic, with the Red Cross and private relief agency personnel portrayed as being close to angels in their selfless sacrifice to assist the victims. The increasing military involvement brings patriotism into the mix and provides the media with the essential local angle—one day Johnny was hauling cement just down the road, and the next day he was on a plane to some dangerous place to bring relief to the suffering on the other side of the globe.

But no story can sustain itself for more than a few days on heroic sacrifice. There have to be problems and the villains that create them. The villains, however, tend to be the easy targets—the UN bureaucrat who failed to mobilize his agency to respond in time or failed to stand up to the power of the local military authorities. The local military authorities themselves are the other villains of the piece. They create the emergency in the first place, harass relief agency personnel, and make the correspondents' tasks that much harder.

The set-piece story never quite comes to a neat ending. Ultimately, there are more failures than successes—food rots on the docks, the war continues, a new disease ravages the camp—yet the crisis stabilizes. The media leave the relief agencies to struggle with the ongoing crisis, which, though less acute, will be of long duration.

Most humanitarian agencies are perfectly content with this script. They love it because they and their staff are invariably the heroes. The agencies' scramble for media coverage is intense precisely because the results, for them, are more positive and credible than a paid public service announcement. Rarely is a critical glance cast in their direction. By definition, they are noble. There appears to be an unwritten rule in the media to go easy on the relief agencies. If mistakes are made, the relief agencies are less liable because their motives are pure.

Emergency response as morality play, however, is ultimately unsatisfying and works against the long-term interests of the relief agencies. As disaster follows disaster, each following the same script, the public, whose support for the agencies is vital to their survival, loses its capacity to distinguish one disaster from another and one agency from another. "Compassion fatigue" blames the victim and numbs individuals who want to care. Humanitarian agencies are failing in the task of educating the public about the root causes of complex emergencies and the essentials of appropriate responses.

The Missing Elements of the Emergency Story

The issue of building greater capacity to promote a fuller understanding of complex emergencies begs the question: What does the current morality play leave out? Some of the critical missing elements are the following:

Analysis of Root Causes

There is a strong tendency to view all emergencies as if they were the equivalents of natural disasters, beyond the control of people. That is a way of avoiding a serious assessment of the factors that created the crises. Coverage of Somalia and Rwanda is an example of the tendency to report on an immediate emergency and only later to ask the hard questions about the role of outside powers in creating it. The humanitarian agencies are complicit in the failure to examine root causes because their ministrations appear more effective when the problem is famine or immediate suffering rather than protracted conflict or the arms trade, issues that are amenable only to long-term public advocacy—advocacy that most agencies shy away from as "too political."

The image of the starving child prompts immediate action. The problem then becomes defined as a logistical one: we (usually from the North, white, wealthy, charitable) have the goods—the food, medicine, shelter, water supply equipment, or clothing. We want to move those goods from countries with surplus production to the people in distress. The issue becomes, then, what is the most economically efficient way to do so? If that is the question, the answer is obvious: whoever has the best capability to move the goods. In our world, it is now often the military, with its exceptional logistic capability, or large relief agencies, which stand ready with private armies of volunteers and professionals, who jump in and solve the logistical problems of an emergency.

If the fundamental problem is logistical, it is clear what must be done: the military and large relief agencies should be given more capacity; there should be more trained Northern experts; and there should be permanent capability in these agencies able to be mobilized at a moment's notice. And the media should focus on reporting the efficiency of the distribution system. Did the supplies reach the scene of the emergency expeditiously? Did they keep the children alive?

Given the slowness and inefficiency of the typical emergency response, these questions can be important and need to be asked. But, fundamentally, they miss the mark. For the problem has been defined by people in the United States or Europe and solved to fit their own needs and requirements. The solutions perpetuate myths and stereotypes, which make long-term change and development more difficult, if not impossible.

The definition of the problem merely as a logistical exercise puts the helper at the center of the process and treats the person to be helped as the dependent victim. Other approaches, however, put the victims of the emergency at the center of the process, which promotes the building of local capabilities and minimizes local vulnerabilities in dealing with the root causes of an emergency. There is a growing literature on the need to keep development principles at the heart of any emergency response, yet the actual practice of the relief community continues to emphasize the heroic outsider providing sustenance to the helpless victim.[1]

Credibility of the Relief Agencies

Rather than creating a halo over every relief agency, the media must begin to ask hard questions about the actual credibility and capacity of agencies to respond to a particular crisis. How many agencies stayed in Somalia from 1989 onward, when conditions were deteriorating and the world was looking elsewhere? How many agencies had given a moment's thought to Rwanda before 1994? Which agencies have real, on-the-ground experience in the country in question, and which are interlopers, trying to grab publicity without the requisite expertise? Which agencies intend to stay and work to build local capacity for the long term, and which will leave within one week of the departure of the last television camera? What mechanisms of providing aid will insure the transition from relief to rehabilitation to long-term development?

Then there are the essential political questions: Which agencies are willing to take public policy positions on the root causes of an emergency? Who is working closely with the military and why are they doing so? Is aid being used to bring about change or to stifle change? Is aid benefiting one political faction?

In an emergency situation local power relationships are often altered, and change is possible. It is crucial that from the outset of relief work, its impact on long-term development (social, cultural, political, and economic) should be weighed. Viewed from a long-term perspective, the responsibility of relief agencies is to work for change side-by-side with local people who are trying to transform the power relationships in a given society for the concrete benefit of the poor. In this context, relief agencies have a responsibility to go beyond their own limited expertise and knowledge and to rely on local human and material resources to take advantage of the opportunities for change presented by an emergency and its attendant upheaval.

Local Capacity

The relief agencies know from experience that the success of any emergency response ultimately depends on the creation of local capacity. Indeed, the fundamental story of emergency response should always begin and end with the tremendous courage of suffering people to struggle against their situation and create a new life and new possibilities. To their credit, the print media, especially, have begun to make progress in this area. Coverage of Rwanda, for example, featured compelling articles on Rwandan human rights workers trying to save hundreds of people from mass slaughter and on Rwandan doctors working in the refugee camps.

The relief agencies prefer to have coverage of disaster response focus on foreigners flying in to rescue anonymous victims, because this story line has the greatest public relations and fundraising payoff for the agencies. However, because these stories ignore the valiant efforts of local people to respond to the immediate emergency, the media should seek out and highlight examples of successful self-help efforts at the local level. This task is especially challenging because of the massive numbers of victims and because of language barriers. As a result, television reporters must rely far too heavily on foreign relief personnel for commentary and interpretation.

Often the most efficient emergency delivery system rides roughshod over local agencies, local experts, local customs, local culture, and local capacities. In the rush to help, foreign relief agencies often will overlook the fact that every society has coping mechanisms for disasters. Societies have institutions that often can be used and strengthened. In the short term this effort may be less efficient than bringing in outside experts (defined logistically), but in the longer term it will build capacity for sustainability.

Responding to an emergency, therefore, is not just moving food, medicines, shelter, and other supplies from point A to point B. Emergency relief is part of a process of development that began before the disaster and that will continue afterward. The best disaster response is carried out by people who have been involved in the development process from an early stage and plan to be involved in the long-term development process after the peak of the crisis. Unfortunately, neither the media nor many international relief agencies have this commitment.

The Rwandan Emergency

The 1994 Rwandan emergency provides an excellent example of the approach of the media and the relief agencies to a complex emergency. It illustrates both the inherent difficulties in making a complex emergency comprehensible to the public and the weaknesses of the media and the relief agencies in overcoming these difficulties.

Rwanda was virtually unknown to the American people before 1994. It was no one's fault. It is a small country on a continent about which Americans are for the most part shamefully ignorant. Few if any U.S. strategic or political interests have ever been at stake in Rwanda. Prior to the emergency, USAID had a modest $19.4 million program there, of which $15.8 million was PL480 food assistance. The Peace Corps, which is still the primary means by which Americans gain direct experience of village-level reality in Africa, had a relatively small program there in the 1970s and 1980s; thirty-two volunteers were present in the country when the program was shut down in 1993 due to increased unrest.

The mass killings in Rwanda, triggered by the crash under mysterious circumstances of the plane carrying presidents Juvenal Habyarimana of Rwanda and Cyprien Ntaryamira of Burundi, received ample coverage in the media despite the overall lack of awareness of the country prior to the violence. The challenge of the 1990s is precisely that the media are able to reach and report on virtually all political and humanitarian emergencies with remarkable swiftness. No relief agency or politician can use lack of knowledge as an excuse for inaction. This is a tremendous advance compared to the two or three previous decades and reflects the impact of the television media's global reach.

The ignorance of the situation in Rwanda among many members of the media, however, did play a decisive role in the way the genocide was covered. In common with coverage of other conflicts in Africa, such as the "black on black" violence in South Africa, the media coverage of the crisis in Rwanda was heavily weighted toward the view that the genocide in Rwanda was the result of a tribal conflict between the Hutu and the Tutsi, the two groups whose populations are intertwined in central Africa. The sheer brutality and scope of the killings, powerfully encapsulated by the still and video shots of bodies clogging rivers and lakes in the region, coupled with the presentation of the conflict as yet another example of the inevitability of intertribal killing in Africa, left the public numbed and powerless to act. For what use is action if the bloodshed is at once large-scale and inevitable?

Within several weeks of the onset of the massacres, however, those few Americans with experience with Rwanda began to raise their voices. They offered an alternative analysis. One of the more compelling was that of Roger Winter, director of the United States Committee for Refugees:

> It would be an unforgivable mistake to pass off the latest orgy of violence in Rwanda as simply another case of African tribal blood-letting that foreigners can never understand and are powerless to prevent. That fatalistically superficial interpretation of events in Rwanda, prevalent in early media reports, makes it convenient for outsiders to throw up their hands in exasperation and walk away.
>
> Characterizing Rwanda's upheaval as the product of primordial ethnic hatreds misses the point of what is really happening there.
>
> Yes, serious ethnic divisions do exist among Rwanda's seven million ethnic Hutu and ethnic Tutsi, to be sure. But the real instigation of violence in Rwanda is shamelessly political, not ethnic. A privileged clique of extremist military and political leaders is ruthlessly determined to block negotiated reforms that would loosen their exclusive grip on power. They have demonstrated again in the last week that they are willing to kill members of their own ethnic group to achieve their own naked political ends.
>
> They manage to survive and succeed time after time by duping foreign journalists and world leaders into believing that Rwanda's spasms of butchery are little more than the unavoidable by-product of Africa's hot ethnic passions. Don't believe it.[2]

Significantly, at this stage of the Rwanda catastrophe, the voices providing an alternative analysis of root causes and calling for political action to halt the genocide were either human rights organizations (Human Rights Watch/Africa), refugee rights organizations (the United States Committee for Refugees), or relief agencies with a commitment to advocacy (Oxfam United Kingdom and Ireland [UKI] and Médecins Sans Frontières). The traditional relief agencies were largely silent. There was little public pressure for action, but a few agencies did what they could with limited resources, mainly providing emergency assistance to Rwandans fleeing the violence in Tanzania, Uganda, and Burundi.

In May and June 1994, the soldiers of the opposition Rwanda Patriotic Front (RPF) continued their advance through the country, which would ultimately, by the end of July, result in their gaining power inside the country. The international community, represented by the United Nations, failed to provide adequate protection to civilians. In April the UN's peacekeeping forces were drastically reduced at just the wrong moment, when the killings began. Now efforts to reintroduce a sizable UN force that would protect civilians and try to mediate between the opposing armies were hampered by bickering in the UN Security Council over finance, sources of the troops, and their mandate. With Hutu—including those responsible for the killings in April—fleeing the advance of the RPF, concern began to be expressed in late June about the possibility of a massive outflow of refugees into Zaire.

Oxfam UKI, among other agencies, sent personnel to prepare a refugee site in the area around Goma in early July. Their best estimate was that perhaps 200,000 people would cross the border. To the astonishment of the international community, as many as 800,000 Rwandans crossed the border into Zaire within forty-eight hours in the third week in July. The broadcast by the world's television media of so many suffering people crammed into unlivable space, many dying from cholera due to lack of clean water, finally created the critical mass in the public consciousness. It touched off another generous outpouring of relief assistance from the American people.

The difference between the public response to the Rwanda crisis in April and May and that in July is critical to understanding the unholy alliance between the media and the relief agencies. The emergency in April, resulting as it had from "ethnic violence" and lacking the striking image of helpless living victims, failed to galvanize the public. The necessary steps to relieve suffering inside Rwanda demanded tremendous courage and political will: courage to try to operate in chaotic and dangerous conditions and the political will simultaneously to call for international political action by the United Nations to reintroduce peacekeeping forces and to initiate steps to identify and bring to justice those responsible for genocide. Political will was also needed to mobilize material support for the new Rwandan government. In these measures the relief community, with a few exceptions, fell considerably short, and the media, lacking the images needed to mobilize the public, were unable to elucidate the crisis in a way that clarified the failures of the United Nations and the relief community.

Thus, when the human tide of Rwandans flooded into Zaire in late July, few asked the tough questions about whether this disaster could have been prevented. The media and the relief agencies went into imme-diate emergency standard operating mode, applying the simplistic moral-ity play formula described above. This benefited the relief agencies by deflecting attention from their collective failure to reduce suffering inside Rwanda from April onward and their unwillingness to speak out on the related critical political questions facing the world community. Now the agencies could pour into Goma, buoyed by the publicity they were receiving and by resulting public donations. Agencies that had done nothing about the Rwanda situation before July 20 were suddenly flying relief teams and equipment into the camps, ready to relieve the suffering of the helpless victims.

The bitter irony in the case of Rwanda, however, is that the relief effort, generally portrayed as a noble success, has had the effect of strengthening the political control over the refugees of the militant Hutu faction responsible for the genocide that created the emergency. Yet there has been virtually no revisiting of the Rwanda story, even by print media, and few in the general public are aware of the unintended but foreseeable impact of the emergency operation in Zaire.

The United Nations

There is one other key international player in an emergency: the United Nations. But the United Nations as the United Nations never responds to emergencies. In truth, a phalanx of UN agencies responds to emergencies—those focused on refugees and those focused on food, health, development, children, peacekeeping, and so on. Each agency comes to the emergency with its own mandate, its own budget, and its own agenda. Some UN agencies have a history in the country; others do not. Usually one agency is designated to coordinate an emergency effort and runs into all the commonplace institutional battles over resources and responsibility.

The Department of Humanitarian Affairs of the United Nations was established in 1992 to help coordinate humanitarian response efforts. Even though it was established with the blessing of and is under the direct supervision of the secretary general, it has not been given the mandate or budget to do its job. If one single capability needs to be developed to help international relief efforts, it is the consolidation of UN agencies (including the merger of some and disappearance of others) and the strong coordination of United Nations emergency efforts by an empowered Humanitarian Affairs office. The disorganization, duplication of tasks, and institutional rivalries that burden the United Nations' relief efforts need to be tackled. In a particular emergency one UN agency or person in the field needs to be given a strong mandate to coordinate, act, and speak on behalf of the United Nations. These changes would have a profound effect not only on those who suffer from disasters but also on the private agencies and the media that flock to them.

Capacity Building: Toward a New Framework for Emergency Response

As the preceding analysis makes clear, lack of information about complex emergencies in and of itself is not the problem. Indeed, once a disaster starts in a way that makes for compelling television, there is an avalanche of information. The problem is the analytical framework that organizes the information provided. The script of the morality play is tired and misleading. A new structure is required that is based on greater knowledge of the countries in question, greater reliance on local resources, and a much sharper critical edge on the part of both the media and the relief agencies.

These improvements must be self-generated. The public has made no demand for change. Indeed, the public is largely uninterested in the root causes of complex emergencies. They accept morality plays as fact.

The incentive for improvements lies more with the relief agencies than with the media. Public cynicism about the efficacy of emergency response will continue to grow unless understanding of the root causes of complex emergencies grows exponentially. Again, "compassion fatigue," to the extent that it exists, is a rational response of the public to the constant repetition of the same story in the same places. Hope—generated from real understanding of the tough issues the poor of the global South are facing and the solutions required to confront these issues—is a more sustainable motive for giving than pity. It is in the self-interest of the most responsible relief agencies to encourage the media to present a more accurate view of the realities that they confront.

New Approach: The Media

Train correspondents to cover issues, activities, and crises in developing countries.

Some academic work or practical experience regarding issues of poverty, civil society, and the politics of the global South should be a requirement for foreign correspondents. Reporting beats on the domestic front almost always require that journalists have a fundamental knowledge of what they are covering, be it government, politics, health, or science. This is not the case with disaster reporting. On an even more fundamental level, journalists given overseas assignments—even when parachuting into a disaster—should be fluent in the language favored locally.

Differences of culture and norms between the global North and South often prevent journalists from understanding local dynamics and make it difficult to go about developing reliable local sources. Instead, they disproportionately depend on others from the North—journalists, UN and diplomatic staff, and aid agency workers.

Create more independence between U.S. journalists and the U.S. State Department and UN officials.

Historically, the media have followed the lead of the U.S. State Department in determining the significance of news around the world. The independence of the media as the "fourth estate" is often lost when dealing with issues overseas. The media focus on events occurring in countries that receive the greatest U.S. foreign aid assistance. These patterns resulted in the media's arriving belatedly to cover the 1984 Ethiopia famine and the recent crises in Somalia and Rwanda.

In fact, Mohamed Amin, the cameraman responsible for presenting the images from Ethiopia in 1984, remains highly critical of the selective behavior of decision-makers in news operations. As we should all recall, the horrific images of the 1984 Ethiopian famine were rejected by both European and U.S. news outlets before the BBC and NBC reversed their decisions.

In talking to news editors and producers, humanitarian agencies often hear that the media cannot lead on these stories. But of course they can, and they did in July 1994, when they provided images of Rwandan refugees dying by the thousands. These activities came in advance of a commitment of U.S. government assistance.

Apply some semantic standards when describing situations outside the United States.

Why is the fighting in Bosnia called an ethnic clash while in Rwanda and other African countries the term is tribal warfare? Furthermore, often there is no discernible difference between power-hungry political leaders everywhere and the "warlords" of Somalia. Yet the media make these and other semantic distinctions and in doing so perpetuate barriers between people in the United States and those outside its borders.

Present the daily lives of people in developing countries and their organized efforts to solve their own problems— before, during, and after crises.

Granted, editors say positive news makes for bad news, but the information-hungry public deserves a full representation of what is going on in the world. A 1:1 ratio of bad news to positive news stories will not, nor should, ever be achieved. But television and print journalists can certainly improve on the present situation. More human interest stories from developing countries would allow the public to develop more realistic impressions of some of our global neighbors. Such stories will also provide a greater understanding of international events and a greater capacity for the public to support U.S. government and private foreign initiatives.

News directors and editors should resist the trend toward celebrity-driven tabloid news that squeezes out news coverage from around the world. (It is not good enough to have to wait for the likes of Michael Jackson visiting Romania to point the news cameras in that direction.)

No one would dispute the fact that the global economy has eliminated borders and widened our horizons in areas of trade and commerce. With those difficult barriers removed, we should seek to eliminate impediments that have created misunderstandings of cultural and societal differences. The conventional wisdom is that the public does not care about issues in other countries. That premise should be challenged. Without access to basic information, how does the public know what it does not care about?

Understandably, among the greatest restrictions to fulfilling these objectives are financial resources. But as CNN and others have proven, identifying and cultivating local journalists as stringers can be effective.

Perhaps the most widely circulated example of a balanced look at the world can be found in the *Los Angeles Times*'s weekly section, the World Report, which offers background pieces on international issues, including positive reporting on development issues. CNN, which has had a profound impact on bringing the world closer to home, also provides viewers more positive stories, most notably during its weekly broadcast, *The World Report*, which is a mixture of stories presented by independent journalists around the world. Ted Turner has introduced another network in the United States, called CNN International, which focuses exclusively on foreign reporting.

These are the most prominent examples of moving beyond reactive foreign reporting. Certainly, there is room for these approaches in other news operations throughout the country. Among the most lamentable situations are the financially strapped PBS efforts of Daniel Schechter, first with the program *South Africa NOW!* and most recently with *Rights and Wrongs*. These were two highly acclaimed efforts to bring enterprising foreign reporting to a U.S. audience. Both have been vexed by limited funding and outspoken and vigilant ideological opposition.

Avoid clichéd, stereotyped reporting.

This is an obvious appeal, but one that merits repeating. Because of the imbalance of bad news from the global South, news editors and producers have the tendency to perpetuate stereotypes and to stigmatize certain groups from this region. In an effort to avoid this and to provide balanced, accurate news, news managers must consider how to follow the intense coverage of a crisis with periodic follow-up reports as well as long-term progress accounts. Ethiopia provides a good example. Once the epitome of independence in Africa, it became the embodiment of dependence following the massive famines of 1974 and 1984. In 1994, exactly ten years after the great 1984 famine, however, Ethiopia was successful in thwarting a potentially devastating food shortage despite the recurrence of similar climatic circumstances. Through the strength of Ethiopians at the community level, the absence of civil war, and a more responsive government and international community, the crisis was averted. Yet there was no story, although millions of people who had supported famine relief activities in 1984 deserved to hear it. And the Ethiopians, too often presented as helpless, deserved to have their self-reliance portrayed accurately in the press.

In May 1994, the respected publication *The Economist* accompanied a story about the country's first-ever multiparty parliamentary elections with a photo of a small malnourished child next to a water container. Including this photograph to highlight a story about strides toward democracy did the country a great disservice; apparently even democracy in Ethiopia can be represented by food and water deficiencies.

News organizations also rely too heavily on stereotypical images, most notably those of starving babies and masses of people, feeding bowls in hand, waiting to be served food. And while these images will probably always be transmitted, we should also challenge photographers to be more creative and innovative.

Increase professional exchange programs between
U.S. and international journalists.

This practice of exchanging journalists from the North and South brings a rich understanding to the business of news gathering. Exchange programs often expose the wide differences in methods of news gathering, government censorship, and techniques in developing reliable sources in various societies.

Do not lose sight of the human aspects of
humanitarian efforts.

Today most crises are being resolved with some aspect of military intervention. In turn the media have begun to cover these missions like the military maneuvers that they are. The image of the Navy Seals coming ashore in Mogadishu will probably become one of the clichéd images from an emergency situation. But no matter how heroic the Marines were, the story should have stayed focused on the people and the local dynamics that created the crisis. There are already some who say the swirling helicopters have replaced starving babies as the "icon" of humanitarian missions. While the military aspect is important, especially when placed in political context, the point is not to be diverted from the story of local people struggling to overcome the crisis in question, including their interaction with and response to the intervening power.

A New Responsibility: The Relief Agencies

Media representatives from relief agencies must be resources for credible analyses of a crisis rather than for the promotion of individual agencies.

The ethic of the relief agencies' interaction with the media should be based on gaining credibility and attendant publicity by providing sound analysis. Agencies should be prepared to provide substantive background information about the local area and the root causes of a crisis. They should also be prepared to direct journalists to local stories, even at the expense of the visibility and identity of their own organizations.

Agencies must reduce their competition for media coverage.

Some competition for media coverage is inevitable in the intense early days of an emergency, when frequent and favorable mention either in print or on television can mean thousands of extra dollars for relief organizations. At the same time, the agencies need to retain perspective and recognize that the portrayal of as complete and accurate a picture of the emergency situation as possible will ultimately be in the interests of the local communities, the agencies, and the public in the home countries. Just as operational cooperation in the field is critical, so is information-sharing and building common positions on key issues. Joint press conferences and statements add weight and credibility to the agencies in their relations with the media.

Relief agencies must promote local capacity, even during a crisis.

Agency public relations representatives and field staff should strive to identify knowledgeable local people to serve as reliable sources. When possible, agencies should also identify local residents who can be hired as translators and assistants for journalists.

The public relations officials of the relief agencies should be sensitive to the ways in which local people are portrayed in the media and should take responsibility for promoting the dignity and capacity of local people. The heartrending images of starving Ethiopians and cholera-ravaged Rwandans will stay etched for a lifetime in the minds of television viewers. Consequently, relief agencies must make all necessary efforts through the media to emphasize the strength, dignity, and intelligence of the people as well.

Agency public relations representatives should have experience in the country in question or, at the very least, some field experience.

The public relations staff of the agencies usually arrive on the scene with journalists. Hence, what is created is a carefully orchestrated operation that could almost be played out in a Hollywood back lot. As the newly arrived journalists meet up with the recently imported agency executives and public relations staff, the rest of the activity becomes almost a backdrop. The agency staff dealing with the media need the knowledge and credibility that come with frequent exposure to complex emergencies, and the perspective, in order to draw the lessons from and point out the unique aspects of the given situation.

Relief agencies have to avoid using emotion-charged pleas that depict beneficiaries as helpless and feeble.

Just as the media continue to rely on stereotypical images, so the relief agencies continue to perpetuate the images of helplessness and despondence among the beneficiaries of the work. This compulsion is not limited to fringe agencies with marginal reputations and effectiveness. Throughout 1994, Save the Children, one of the oldest and most respected of the development and relief agencies in the United States, ran a print ad campaign that featured, in succession, a Sudanese child menaced by a vulture, two dead Somali children, and a tight closeup of a starving child. While such images are powerful, and certainly tug on the heartstrings, they fail utterly to reflect the strength and dignity of the beneficiaries. Indeed, such images abuse the agencies' privileged access to other peoples' suffering. Save the Children's campaign added insult to injury in that the photos used in the campaign were stock photos from news organizations that bore no direct relationship to the actual people or communities with which the organization was working.

Private U.S. agencies need only live up to the code of conduct developed collaboratively by their umbrella organization, InterAction. It prohibits the use of such images in fundraising.[3]

Relief agencies have to be prepared for greater media scrutiny.

If the media are willing to invest in increasing their capacity to report on the root causes of complex emergencies, relief agencies have to prepare themselves for greater scrutiny. Unfortunately, more than thirty years of disaster reporting has placed the private agencies on the side of the angels. It has not prepared agencies very well for a potential shift in the media's lens. Even minor critiques from the media tend to elicit defensiveness from relief agencies.

For example, in the *New York Times* (December 18, 1994), veteran foreign correspondent Raymond Bonner revisited the Rwandan emergency and assessed the performance of the agencies. His criticisms were mild. He singled out one agency for providing inappropriate supplies, praised the performance of six agencies by name, and concluded, "what the private humanitarian organizations contributed to the well-being of the refugees was not commensurate with the money donated . . . not as many lives were saved as might have been."[4] A press office of a major agency was disappointed that Bonner's story was not more upbeat.

Yet, if the media end their artificial and counterproductive policy of gentleness toward the relief agencies, articles like Bonner's would just be a beginning. Agencies are vulnerable to scrutiny on a number of counts:
— The provision of inappropriate material assistance;
— The youth and inexperience of their staff and volunteers;
— Their inability to plan and coordinate, resulting in waste and duplication of effort;
— Their failure to address root causes and long-term problems;
— Their inability or unwillingness to work with local people; and
— The link between aid provision and proselytizing.

The dependence of many agencies on U.S. government funding is another area of vulnerability. Even in a world without superpower conflict, the United States has narrow political interests and a need to project its power to protect them. Even in emergency situations—sometimes especially in emergency situations—U.S. government funding will reflect a political agenda. Agencies lacking a private financial base—and there are agencies that raise as little as 20 percent of their funds from the public—face the prospect of becoming an instrument of U.S. foreign policy.

Rwanda again is a case in point. For reasons that are difficult to understand but that were based on an assessment of U.S. interests in the region, in 1994 the United States provided virtually no funding to the new Rwandan government after it had established control over the bulk of the territory and population of the country. This decision, reminiscent of the overt embargo against the government of Cambodia in the 1980s, meant that, while agencies working with refugees outside of Rwanda were well-funded, few agencies were able to work inside the country. Yet, because most agencies do not believe in doing political advocacy, they simply accepted this discrepancy. In the meantime, the Rwandan people inside the country suffered.

Thus, the media should be asking the following questions of the relief agencies: How independent are they? How much does their work diverge from that of the U.S. government? Do the agencies work only through groups (or governments) supported by the U.S. government? Are the agencies willing to advocate positions contrary to those of the U.S. government?

Conclusion

In the dynamic relationship among the media, relief agencies, and the public, the relief agencies that fail to modify their programs and public relations efforts will be increasingly vulnerable to criticism from more knowledgeable and vigilant media reporting of emergency situations. They will gain, however, from an aggressive and honest examination of their strengths and weaknesses, followed by changes in their operations and the way that they seek to have them portrayed. This conclusion therefore focuses on the relief agencies.

The number of agencies that flock to disasters from all over the global North is staggering. Even in countries where emergencies are not well publicized, such as Mali and the Gambia, the number of international relief and development agencies competing is difficult to justify. The tendency is for each to come in with its own ideas and its own solutions— often manufactured in the North. This is a key problem. In the North people are taught to be problem solvers. If something is broken, fix it. If food needs to be delivered somewhere, figure out the best and the most efficient way to do so.

In emergencies, as in development, the best approach often is not to act but to listen, not to ride roughshod over local capacity but to be patient in finding local capacity and then building on it. *But this requires a reeducation of relief agency personnel, a redefinition of what is success, and a reformulation of strategies and processes for effective action.*

Non-governmental agencies will have to develop local capacities, strengthening local organizations and transferring to local people more and more responsibility for operations. Ultimately, international relief agencies should operate only through local organizations and local channels.

Local capacities need to be developed before a crisis arrives. The most effective relief work would therefore be capacity- and institution-building and training, so that local societies could organize for their own emergencies, accepting funds and food from the outside and managing their own response. This new approach needs to be at the focal point of the work of relief agencies. Unfortunately, most are so busy putting out fires that they are not focused on long-term solutions.

Until such time as the international relief agencies are willing to challenge the ways in which they do business and to explore alternatives that put not themselves but the so-called victims in the center of the process, then capacity-building within these northern agencies will not address fundamental issues.

It is equally important for non-governmental agencies to be vigilant as to who is falling through the cracks in any and every relief situation. This is best explained by looking at the United States. The United States is often struck with emergencies—witness Hurricane Andrew, the floods in the Midwest, and the earthquake in Los Angeles, all within a twelve-month period. Non-governmental agencies mobilized to send in relief supplies; the federal government, through the Federal Emergency Management Agency and others, responded with money. In each case the media reported on the immediate impact of this assistance. But in each of these three emergencies, many people, particularly the poor and racial minorities, fell through the cracks of assistance. Even with the amount of aid flowing to those disasters in one of the richest countries in the world, poor people did not receive adequate benefits.

If another hurricane hits the Louisiana coast or the fields in Florida, those left dispossessed the last time will suffer again because private relief agencies, the government, and the media did not learn appropriately from the disasters; relief programs still do not reach the most marginal people. Thus, even in the United States relief strategies are flawed because we do not listen well to the people in need. Programs are designed by bureaucrats or outsiders. Relief agencies are not asking how to best address the reasons for people's vulnerability in the first place.

Non-governmental agencies must learn how to deal with root causes and design programs that respond to the real needs of marginal populations.

Relief agencies need to advocate changes in government relief efforts and United Nations policies. Governments have political agendas that often fly in the face of effective long-term relief. In these instances, non-governmental agencies need to speak out. As much as possible this advocacy should be based on a detailed knowledge of the suffering experienced by certain groups and the views of the leaders of local communities who have articulated their needs and demands to the wider world. This is a tremendous responsibility and demands skill and sensitivity from agency personnel.

Advocacy can begin with basic issues. For example, governmental support should help to create and expand governmental and local NGO early warning systems. They have proved invaluable, for example in Southern Africa and Ethiopia, in marshaling resources in time for relief.

Non-governmental agencies need to advocate a stronger United Nations Department of Humanitarian Affairs and a restructuring of the United Nations relief agencies. A strong, unified, and coordinated United Nations would add significant capability to the international relief effort. The United Nations would need to articulate and promote early warning systems, emergency response, and rehabilitation and recovery. Further, only the United Nations has the capacity, potentially, to link emergency responses to political actions to mitigate humanitarian crises on behalf of the international community.

Relief work is challenging. The responsibility of relief agencies is immense. If done correctly, relief can be a step in building a sustainable society. In a relief situation, existing power relationships are often broken; these situations therefore provide an opportune time for change. Relief must be viewed not as the end product but rather as a crucial step on a long road. Doing so can help change communities and society. Ultimately, the goal of relief work is not merely to keep people alive; it is to be a key part of a process of societal rebuilding and transformation.

Relief agencies and the media have a crucial role to play in this drama. Either they can support stereotypes that reinforce patterns of domination and dependence, or they can opt to be part of the process of positive, sustainable change. Doing so will require breaking bad habits built up over a period of time. It will require changes in the way the media cover emergencies. It will mean breaking the unholy alliance of NGOs and the media, which often works against long-term sustainable change. And it will mean recognizing that the main actors in the drama of building sustainable societies are neither the private relief agencies nor the media but rather the people and institutions of society. The local people must become the catalysts for sustainable development.

Notes

1. Mary B. Anderson and Peter J. Woodrow, *Rising from the Ashes: Development Strategies in Times of Disaster* (Boulder, Colo., 1989). See also Frederick C. Cuny, *Disasters and Development* (Dallas, 1994), the reprinting of a volume originally published in 1983; John Osgood Field (ed.), *The Challenge of Famine: Recent Experience, Lessons Learned* (West Hartford, Conn., 1994).

2. Roger Winter, "Slaughter in Rwanda: It's More Politics Than Tribalism," *Monday Developments,* 12 (April 25, 1994), 8–9.

3. *InterAction Standards* state in part, "Fund raising solicitations shall be truthful. . . . There shall be no material omissions or exaggerations of fact, no use of misleading photographs, nor any other communication which would tend to create a false impression or misunderstanding. . . . An organization's communications shall respect the dignity, values, history, religion, and culture of the people served by the programs."

4. Raymond Bonner, "Compassion Wasn't Enough in Rwanda," *New York Times* (December 18, 1994), D3.

CHAPTER SIX

The Media and the Refugee

Lionel Rosenblatt

A COMMON THREAD runs through the humanitarian crises involving the flight of Kurds from Iraq in 1991, the starvation of Somalis in 1992, the shelling of Sarajevo in 1993 and 1995, and the slaughter of Rwandans in 1994. A different common thread is present in a second group of humanitarian emergencies: war, chaos, and suffering in Azerbaijan, the Sudan, Angola, and Liberia. What makes these situations different from those in the first list?

The answer is prime-time television news coverage of the Kurds, Somalis, Sarajevans, and Rwandans. The troubles in Azerbaijan, the Sudan, Angola, and Liberia received relatively little coverage.

It is no accident that the international response to the first group of emergencies was faster, more massive, and more successful than it was for the second group. The so-called "CNN factor" was the difference. Television created a constituency for the victims of one group of emergencies, fostering among all of us a feeling of responsibility for their fate and causing world leaders to try to alleviate the horrible scenes of inhumanity that we were seeing every night on our television screens. It is interesting that in the four emergencies we identified in which media coverage was heavy, the international response was military. In Somalia, Rwanda, and Iraq, the United States mounted a military rescue operation. In Bosnia, the military response came from NATO airstrikes against rebel Serbian forces shelling civilians in the city of Sarajevo.

However, we should not too readily accept the fact that the critical elements in meeting a humanitarian emergency are heavy television coverage and U.S. military intervention. In all of the cases cited, media coverage and military intervention were too little, too late, or too ineffectual to prevent a heavy loss of lives. A brief look at each of the examples illustrates the shortcomings of the international response to each emergency.

In Iraq, the flight of the Kurds was caused by the use of force by President Saddam Hussein against his own citizens in an attempt to remain in power despite his military defeat at the hands of the allied forces. The result was a surge of over 1 million Kurdish refugees into mountainous border areas to escape Saddam's military forces. More decisive military action by the United States and its allies at the conclusion of Operation Desert Storm and in support of the Shiite and Kurd rebellions might have prevented a humanitarian crisis. Once the Kurds fled to the remote mountains along the Iraqi-Turkish border, it was primarily media attention that moved the United States into a rescue operation by the U.S. military.

In Somalia, the United States ruled out participation in a UN peacekeeping mission. The United States sent its military forces to Somalia in order to feed the starving people who were seen dying on TV screens every night. We were successful in achieving this limited objective but failed to effect the larger political reforms that might have resolved the ongoing crisis. Media coverage created a constituency for military intervention but also served to undermine that constituency. The American decision to leave Somalia was made in response to public outcry after a bloody attack on U.S. troops in October 1993 received extensive coverage on television. The pictures of the corpse of a U.S. soldier being dragged through the streets caused the American public to react with horror.

Television pictures of the gory shelling of Sarajevo's market in 1993, in which more than sixty people died, and Peter Jennings's interview with Fred Cuny and his immediate and graphic reporting from the scene stimulated a forthright NATO and UN response to rebel Bosnian Serb attacks on civilian populations. The UN commander was given authority to call for NATO airstrikes to punish violations of the UN-declared "heavy weapons exclusion zones" and "safe areas." NATO intervention, however, proved cosmetic until 1995, when another well-publicized shelling of Sarajevo stimulated a NATO bombing campaign that helped force the Serbs to the bargaining table.

In Rwanda, there was too little media coverage and it came too late to have any effect in halting the mass murder of half a million people. The international community failed to respond appropriately, in part because at the time of the outbreak of violence there were too few television crews in the country to capture the unprecedented scope and scale of the slaughter. Once the enormity of the genocide was discovered, almost no TV crews dared to enter Rwanda. It was only belatedly, as a result, that television pictures of dying refugees mobilized world public opinion. A U.S. military rescue mission was then launched in response to public opinion and—as Rwanda slipped off the front pages—the military mission was quietly terminated.

The point of these illustrations is that the CNN factor—heavy media coverage of humanitarian emergencies—proved a critical influence on policy-makers. They took meaningful action, including military intervention, to save hundreds of thousands of lives in Iraq, Somalia, Bosnia, and Rwanda. Without media attention, governments and international organizations probably would not have responded as quickly and massively as they did. However, neither media attention nor the intervention of the international community in these humanitarian emergencies resulted in complete success.

This chapter examines the influence that the media have in stimulating public policy-makers to take action in humanitarian emergencies. My thesis is that the media have a great deal of short-term influence in creating an instant constituency for appropriate action. They influence policy-makers to put an issue on the top of their agendas. The influence of the media can be harnessed by humanitarian organizations to encourage effective international action to meet the urgent needs of victims of humanitarian disasters.

The second part of my thesis, however, is that the media pay little attention to long-term problems and thus have little interest or influence in preventing or ameliorating humanitarian emergencies. The corollary to this statement is that humanitarian organizations must work to develop a more predictive and preventive outlook by public policy-makers, the media, and the public in general.

In today's world of satellite television transmission and information superhighways, most major world events unfold in the glare of publicity. An aphorism, flippant but to a certain extent apt, might be that if a humanitarian emergency is not featured in the media, it does not become an emergency for political leaders and policy-makers. Policy-makers focus on the problems brought to their immediate attention, and one of the most potent means of bringing problems to their attention is through media coverage. The examples of the humanitarian crises in Azerbaijan, the Sudan, Angola, and Liberia illustrate the point. Because these difficult humanitarian concerns have not had media attention, world leaders have not had to address them as priorities.

The media are, of course, diverse. The use of the term in this chapter refers to that segment of daily reportage that is brought to the direct attention of public policy-makers or, in other words, the words and pictures that international policy-makers read or see during the day. What media outlets have the most influence?

The reading and viewing habits of State Department officials are probably typical of most policy-makers in Washington. Every morning at seven, its Operations Center produces a daily news summary for policy-makers that consists of relevant press clips from the *New York Times*, the *Washington Post*, the *Washington Times*, the *Baltimore Sun*, the *Wall Street Journal*, and the *Christian Science Monitor*. The stories in those newspapers focus attention on new issues and developments that may require action during the day. (The press clips are not, of course, the policy-maker's only or most important source of information. Intelligence summaries, reports from foreign posts, and information from a wide variety of other sources will also be used to help make decisions.)

The television viewing of the policy-makers is more diverse and difficult to quantify. CNN, of course, may be the most watched news network because it can be tuned in at any time of the day or night. The evening news shows of the three major networks are not widely watched, except in times of fast-moving crises, because most policy-makers are working at the time they are aired. *The MacNeil/Lehrer NewsHour* is probably official Washington's most watched news program because it examines the issues of the day in more detail than do the networks.

My impression is that policy-makers utilize print journalism primarily as a source of background information and ideas. Television, on the other hand, makes them aware of the issues to which they must react immediately whether they want to or not.

I claim that media attention plays an important role in influencing public policy toward humanitarian emergencies only. I do not claim, nor do I believe, that the media outlets cited above have any overwhelming, or even important, influence over most other issues of public policy. I doubt, for example, that the *Washington Post* has any significant influence over the outcome of elections in any of the fifty states or, for that matter, in Washington, D.C. However, in narrowly focused situations such as humanitarian emergencies, the media play a decisive role in informing the public and stimulating action.

Nor am I advocating a short-term media strategy as a substitute for the long-term development of a public constituency for humanitarian organizations and assistance to people in need wherever they may be. For humanitarian organizations, media attention can only serve as a supplement to the grass-roots support of millions of people. The nature of my own organization, Refugees International, leads me to focus on the media and their role in alleviating human disasters.

Refugees International is an advocacy organization that works on behalf of refugees and displaced persons around the world. We are not in the nuts-and-bolts business of delivering goods and services to needy people. Rather, we have the more nebulous task of trying to ensure that policy-makers, the public, and relief organizations are made aware of humanitarian emergencies at the earliest possible moment in order to encourage early and effective action to reduce human suffering.

The media, therefore, are our natural allies. We operate on the assumption that media attention to humanitarian tragedies will expand a public constituency in favor of helping the victims, and influence policy-makers to act more quickly and allocate greater resources to a problem.

It is a source of both pride and concern that non-governmental organizations (NGOs) have a powerful influence in generating media coverage in humanitarian emergencies. Somalia is a good example. The UN and its member states had largely abandoned Somalia in the early 1990s. The situation was considered too dangerous and too difficult to deal with by the international community. It fell by default to the international non-governmental organizations in Somalia, primarily humanitarian relief organizations, to focus the world's attention on the plight of Somalis. The rescue mission ultimately carried out by the United States was in response to a public constituency created by media attention.

From my own experience, media reporting can have a positive impact in humanitarian emergencies. In the spring of 1993, Refugees International was alerted by a UN source that the relief pipeline for food to Sarajevo was virtually exhausted. I immediately traveled to the UN complex on the Bosnian-Croatian border and was able to confirm the incredible fact that the warehouses were empty. I returned to Sarajevo and sought out a *New York Times* reporter of my acquaintance. He was, as I was, astounded by my finding and immediately went to work on a story that appeared on the Monday after Easter. Within a few days, over

$30 million in contributions was pledged by the U.S. and European governments, and the UN made an all-out effort to replenish its food stocks. A major interruption to Sarajevo's food pipeline was avoided. The media, by embarrassing governments and the UN over this preventable situation, caused policy-makers to react immediately to solve the problem.

In the examples of Somalia and Bosnia cited above, media receptivity was greatly enhanced by the credibility of the NGOs and their representatives and by their personal contacts with journalists. Credibility is the essential element if NGOs are to influence the media and policy-makers.

The examples above illustrate ways in which the media have been effective in influencing development of public policies to assist victims of humanitarian disasters. But the media also have limitations.

First, the media, especially television, report what is currently happening but are not very interested in covering anticipated events. If we were to contact the media to tell them that a possible 10,000 people could be murdered in country X tomorrow, I doubt that such a prediction would receive much attention. On the other hand, if we were to contact our friends in the media and tell them that 10,000 people are being murdered today in country X, we would elicit much more interest. Because television relies on graphic images for its influence, evocative and emotional reporting on humanitarian disasters usually happens only after immense loss of life and property occurs.

Second, in this day of pervasive media presence, a lack of coverage of a humanitarian crisis may lead the public to sense that the problem cannot really be very serious if it is not broadcast on their television screens in the evening. Moreover, if the suppression of the Kurds or Shiites in Iraq after Desert Storm had appeared on television sooner, we might have been catalyzed to take more effective, earlier action on their behalf. It was not until the Kurds fled into the mountains and the international media got access to them that we began to see the pictures of their suffering and that a public constituency developed in favor of assisting them.

Another example of the difference the presence of the media can make is in the cases of the Sudan and Somalia. The scope and scale of human suffering is at least as great in the Sudan as in Somalia, and the human tragedy has endured longer in the Sudan and appears less amenable to easy amelioration. The media have been absent in the Sudan, and as a result the majority of the U.S. population is unaware of the humanitarian tragedy in that country. Yet the sight on the nightly news shows of the starving and dying victims of the war in Somalia stimulated a U.S. military intervention with humanitarian objectives.

A third limitation of using the media to help to develop a constituency to address humanitarian emergencies is the media's short-term attention span. Rwanda is a case in point. Soon after the fighting began, I traveled to the area, made an assessment of the crisis caused by a million or more Rwandans fleeing into Zaire to escape the civil strife in their own country, and determined that the potential for massive suffering and loss of life was imminent. Upon my return to the United States, we called a press conference to alert the media about this fast-developing crisis. As a result, this action led to other opportunities to bring the story to the public. Especially helpful was a lengthy discussion on the *MacNeil/Lehrer NewsHour*, during which we were able to document the situation's extreme urgency. This was followed by televised congressional testimony. Working with the media, Refugees International and other advocacy groups were able successfully to encourage the Clinton administration to undertake an emergency military rescue mission for the Rwandan refugees.

A few weeks later Refugees International was back in Africa visiting the refugee camps, which now had almost 2 million inhabitants. The crisis was growing daily, but CNN was gone, the networks were gone, and the reporters whose names are household words were gone. The media presence in Goma consisted of just two wire service reporters. UN officials expressed the fear that once they were gone, the world's support for the UN's humanitarian effort would evaporate. The public's attention, guided and formed by the media, vanished as quickly as had the television cameras.

There is a final point on the media's limitations as catalysts for public policy. The media quickly respond to disasters of major proportions. In Rwanda we saw half a million dead and almost 2 million refugees. Will the media—and the international community—respond as readily and rapidly to a smaller disaster? A danger might arise in comparing future crises with Rwanda, which set the standard for the definition of a "major" disaster. A humanitarian crisis that does not involve such huge numbers of people may be regarded as "minor." If the number of threatened people in the next humanitarian disaster is less than that in Rwanda, will the television cameras and thus policy-makers and the public be as interested? If the number of deaths and refugees total only a few hundred thousand, will the crisis be seen by the media as less urgent and less worthy of their time and attention?

How can humanitarian agencies develop the already existing relationship with the media and use them more effectively to create support for humanitarian action in emergencies?

The challenge of the post–Cold War era is clear. This is an era of proliferating conflicts, both internal and external, and competition among nations for resources. In place of the Cold War competition between the ideologies of the two superpowers, the confrontations of the foreseeable future are likely to be based on ethnic differences and disputes. While the Cold War imposed stability on the world and focused the attention of the superpowers on preventing conflicts and problems from spreading, the instability of newly created governments and the internal ethnic conflicts now occuring in every corner of the world carry the potential for staggering costs in human life and resources.

The number of refugees and displaced persons in the world is at an all-time high: a recent estimate is 23 million refugees and 26 million displaced persons. Few people are so optimistic as to expect that number to decline in the next few years. The likelihood is that the international community will be faced with Rwandas and Bosnias over and over again.

The central lesson we have learned from experience with humanitarian emergencies is that identification of the needs involved in crises and early responses to crises saves lives and resources. A useful media role has been that of publicizing crises already under way. We should look at ways in which the media can help us anticipate humanitarian disasters and help us create a public constituency to undertake preventive measures.

It is much more difficult to engender support among policy-makers and the general public for preventive measures than it is to rally them around an existing crisis. Media stories about preventing disasters do not have the same impact as television coverage of the dead and dying. Since television deals mainly in visual images, it may be that the old-fashioned print media will be our most effective allies in initiating preventive strategies.

As an example of preventive action that should be undertaken, let us look at Rwanda in 1995. We have a crisis waiting to happen—another round of genocidal war. What are we doing to prevent it? The world community should be undertaking a whole range of projects to create more stability in Rwanda. For example, government offices in Kigali often do not possess a pencil to write with or a piece of paper to write on. Basic emergency assistance to the Rwandan government would help it do its job, reassure its people, and promote the return of the displaced and the refugees. However, the world community is not inclined to address these very basic needs. International organizations cite arrearages on previous loans as reasons for holding up assistance to Rwanda. The UN and national government assistance agencies are slow, ponderous, and bureaucratic. A few well-placed stories in well-read newspapers and news magazines could stimulate public support.

Other examples of the kinds of problems getting little or no media attention and thus lacking a public constituency are

— the politically destabilizing activities of a hate radio station which, in 1994, spewed ethnic venom into Rwanda. The international community had not been able to agree that it should be repressed. Nor had it raised the thousands of dollars that it would have taken to purchase jamming equipment;

— the ongoing need for human rights monitors to be stationed in all areas of Rwanda to give comfort to a fearful people;

— the slow process of calling to account those who are guilty of war crimes; and

— the continuing flow of arms to the refugee camps, which makes it possible for refugees to contemplate overthrowing the Rwandan government. This flow should be halted by an international police force if necessary.

Unfortunately, Rwanda disaster Part Two is waiting to happen, and the world in general is unaware of the steps that could be taken to prevent it.

The challenge in this post–Cold War period of ethnic conflicts and instability is to convince the governments of the world to give the same attention to the anticipation and prevention of human disasters as they did to the prevention of superpower conflict during the forty years following World War II. To anticipate and prevent a superpower conflict, the United States kept hundreds of thousands of soldiers stationed in Europe, spent billions of dollars on missile systems and antimissile systems, and spent billions more dollars fighting to control the spread of communism.

The present era deserves a similar effort. We need to undertake an extensive reform of the United Nations so that it can become an effective and efficient instrument of the international community for meeting humanitarian crises. The UN should be the equivalent of a Distant Early Warning (DEW) system, the better to anticipate a crisis in the making. An early monitoring and early response capability and the security forces and resources to move people and materiel to a crisis area are essential. Better coordination among non-governmental organizations, so that their strengths can be matched to the needs of an emergency, is also important. Finally, the media should accept the challenge of providing continuing, daily reporting on the condition of people around the world.

Our challenge, as representatives of humanitarian organizations, is to find ways to use the media to bring information to the public so that they will become educated and motivated advocates for solutions to the humanitarian crises we face today. We must begin to think about new ways to take action to prevent the causes of so much of the human suffering that now results from our failure to anticipate problems and take early action.

Non-governmental organizations must look for ways in which we can join together in a "humanitarian lobby" to influence government policy-makers, international agencies, and public opinion.

There are four ways in which NGOs can build public support:

—Non-governmental organizations can cooperate in new and different ways, as in a recent mission to Burundi by representatives of Search for Common Ground and Refugees International. While Search for Common Ground concentrated on conflict prevention, using such measures as a peace radio, negotiation training, and reconciliation projects, the Refugees International team worked with the UN on the emergency protection and assistance needs of refugees and displaced persons as well as on new ways of meeting the violence that is rampant in the camps. Each organization will work through its own channels to raise awareness of the conditions in Burundi.

—One method of sharing information and ideas that is currently being used for Burma, Tajikistan, and Burundi, is an open-forum round table of all those interested in a particular emergency. This will help to build a critical mass of interest and to centralize accurate, timely information.

—Another possible NGO contribution to media coverage would be to facilitate the preparation of professional quality video coverage of emergencies. The networks could then use it. Perhaps it is time for a new NGO to fill this niche, possibly a "Photographers without Borders."

—Similarly, NGOs might support a reporter function to write about an emergency in the field.

In conclusion, with a view to maintaining interest in a problem long enough to produce creative and effective solutions, it is clear that NGOs in both the assistance and advocacy fields need to be much more conscious of the need to nurture public awareness of humanitarian emergen-

cies. We should find ways to improve our methods of building con-
stituencies in the post-post–Cold War world.

As humanitarian organizations, we need to tell the American people
not only that we feed children in Somalia and treat disease in Angola but
that we also use our expertise and influence to anticipate and prevent
human disasters.

We need to promote the message that helping to anticipate and prevent
humanitarian disasters is a necessity and that a world in which the fundamental human rights of every individual are protected is a better—and
safer—world for us all.

Part Three

IMPROVING U.S. POLICY

CHAPTER SEVEN

Illusions of Influence:
The CNN Effect in Complex Emergencies

Andrew Natsios

THE INCREASE in the number and apparent deadliness of manmade disasters over the past five years has caused policy-makers to focus on the international disaster response system and whether it works well or might be improved. The broader focus of this chapter deals with how such a system is activated to respond—who makes the decision to respond, how the decision is made, and what pressures are brought to bear on the decision-making process. It will not deal with the operation of the response system itself. More specifically, this chapter will examine whether the news media play a central role in forcing public policy-makers to attend to a major foreign disaster and when the media's role is peripheral or irrelevant.

It is readily demonstrable that media coverage of disasters profoundly affects both public opinion and policy-making process.[1] If it is particularly thoughtful and continuous, coverage can educate the public about the developing world and about the consequences of disasters. Media coverage can also serve an important function as a mechanism for raising resources. Non-governmental organizations (NGOs) use this exposure to raise funds privately to manage their disaster response operations. This same exposure encourages Congress to spend more taxpayer dollars on the disaster response—through contributions to governmental, intergovernmental, and non-governmental organizations.

Generally, the longer a disaster continues, the more intense and influential media coverage becomes. This phenomenon is more pronounced in a slow-onset disaster. In a war or famine, the most common types of slow-onset disasters, there are fewer spectacular events to report on than there are in earthquake or volcanic disasters. Famines do not become visually newsworthy until people die, which takes place only in the advanced stages of a drought cycle. The visual nature of television accentuates such differences.

This chapter suggests that the so-called "CNN effect" has taken on more importance than it deserves as an explanation for responses emanating from the policy-making process in Washington. In its crudest form the CNN effect suggests that policy-makers only respond when there are scenes of mass starvation on the evening news. It also suggests that policy-makers obtain most of their information about ongoing disasters from media reports. Both propositions are inaccurate and seriously exaggerated. The truth is that most complex emergencies receive little media coverage at any stage. Usually it is when the disaster response is unsuccessful and people die that serious coverage occurs.

Complex Humanitarian Emergencies

One category of disasters, complex humanitarian emergencies (CHEs), has seen more growth in numbers than any other category in recent years. This term describes emergencies in which four characteristics are present: (1) food insecurity, frequently deteriorating into mass starvation; (2) macroeconomic collapse involving hyperinflation, debasement of a currency, net decreases in GNP, and massive unemployment; (3) ethnic or religious violence, widespread human rights abuses, and the deterioration of central government authority; and (4) mass population displacement. CHEs inevitably lead to a collapse of civil society. According to one study, between 1964 and 1990, famines and civil wars accounted for 75 percent of all deaths in all categories of disasters. Such CHEs accounted for 90 percent of all U.S. government relief expenditures in fiscal 1993.[2] Complex emergencies also pose a challenge to international order and stability because they are not contained by national boundaries. Because of this unique distinguishing characteristic, CHEs have become a focus of foreign policy study. According to one such study, between 1978 and 1985, there were an average of five complex emergencies each year. In 1989, the number grew to fourteen. In 1994, there were twenty. [3]

The interventions needed to save lives in complex emergencies are no mystery: food, medical care, shelter, and clean water and sanitation. NGOs, the International Committee of the Red Cross (ICRC), and the UN specialized agencies can provide these interventions without much notice or difficulty at relatively modest cost if access and delivery of relief assistance to vulnerable populations are not problems. However, access to those in danger has become a heated political issue. All sides in a conflict will typically use the wealth represented in disaster relief commodities—food, medicine, and relief infrastructure—as tools of war. They are used to buy support for one's cause or to deny support to the opposing side. They can be sold and the proceeds used to purchase more weapons. It has become a virtual axiom of complex emergencies that the more severe the economic dislocation caused by a crisis, the greater the relative value of humanitarian relief commodities will become and the more likely that gangs of thugs will attempt to take advantage of them if the combatants do not get to them first. Humanitarian relief is a major source of wealth in armed conflicts and is therefore of enormous interest to the contestants. So access to relief becomes central to disaster response.

Guaranteeing access to victims under these circumstances is no simple matter. Humanitarian organizations have shown little skill in dealing with this problem since it frequently involves intervening militarily, negotiating diplomatic agreements, and implementing other security measures. Some of the anarchy in Somalia was undoubtedly caused by inappropriate security measures employed by relief organizations. These measures made the U.S. military's mission much more difficult when it eventually arrived. Ensuring access in complex emergencies also may involve much larger and politically sensitive issues like the deployment of troops and the expenditure of diplomatic capital to negotiate access agreements. It is when security and diplomatic issues become paramount that media coverage of complex emergencies has the most profound effect on donor governments and the United Nations.

The Office of Foreign Disaster Assistance (OFDA) and Office of Food for Peace (FFP) in the U.S. Agency for International Development (AID) have the lead civilian role in the U.S. government for responding to complex emergencies. They have shown no reluctance to provide humanitarian assistance when emergencies occur, absent Washington's bureaucratic battles on foreign policy issues or problems of access to those at risk. Problems have sometimes arisen when other bureaucratic actors have become involved within the government and the UN. When issues of statecraft, military strategy, and domestic politics are mixed, disaster management becomes considerably more complicated.

The CNN Effect

For many years commentators have drawn a connection between photographs of starving children on the evening news and a more aggressive U.S. policy to combat starvation, even to the point of military intervention—the CNN effect. While it is certainly the case that photojournalism can influence some policy-makers sometimes, what has not been carefully studied is when and how that influence occurs. The relationship between gruesome media reporting and disaster response is by no means exact. Domestic politics, other coincidental foreign policy crises, debate about what is in the national interest, the strategic location of a CHE to other geopolitical interests, and bureaucratic battles over budgets all influence the process. Some disaster responses are undertaken from start to finish with little or no media coverage. This chapter suggests that the CNN effect is of limited consequence, at times playing a supportive but not central role, and at others being a major factor in the decision-making process.

Although some attention has been paid to the role of presidential leadership (or its absence) in mobilizing international responses and to the role of the news media in encouraging that leadership, little analysis has been undertaken of the decision-making machinery absent presidential leadership or media attention. Those within the U.S. foreign policy apparatus (for example, AID and State Department career foreign service officers, Department of Defense officers, and political appointees) play a much greater role in the success or failure of American relief responses than is commonly understood. Timeliness is perhaps the single most important characteristic of a successful response and yet the most problematic. The longer the response is delayed, the more people die. By the time most complex humanitarian emergencies emerge from the gray underworld of our disaster response structure, cable traffic, intelligence reports, and emergency planning, it is sometimes too late for presidential intervention. How the lower levels of the U.S. foreign policy apparatus confront these emergencies is thus of considerable significance.

PROPOSITION I: Policy-makers will actively support an early and robust government humanitarian response to a complex humanitarian

emergency if it threatens the geopolitical interests of the United States. Electronic and print media attention will be tangential or irrelevant to the decision, whether or not the United States intervenes.

During the great Sahelian drought of the mid-1980s, most of the governments in the affected region fell (or nearly fell) from coups d'état as a result of their inability to cope with the drought. Not surprisingly, droughts are destabilizing politically even when they occur without the other characteristics of complex emergencies. If a government cannot even feed its own people in a time of disaster, of what use is it? Complex emergencies, and the political instability that accompanies them, interrupt most other agendas that a U.S. embassy may have in a country. They are not taken lightly.

Career diplomats instinctively avoid instability and unpredictability in diplomatic relationships. New governments may not necessarily mean better official relations with Washington. American ambassadors are judged by foreign service norms, which include their access to senior government officials in the host governments, the general state of relations between the two countries, and the popularity of the United States in the country generally. A national crisis that threatens a large number of lives typically creates a platform for U.S. ambassadors to show their competence. During the Cold War a government's disposition toward the Soviet Union influenced the equation to a marked degree; but now, without that complicating measurement, diplomats normally revert to their inherent conservatism. Even without their visceral attraction to stability and access, they know the human cost of famines. Even if for no other reason than humanitarian, they will call for help. There have been few exceptions to this principle over the past ten years, even when the regimes were disposed toward the Soviet Union. Ambassadorial behavior is of some consequence since, under AID procedures, the mechanism for mobilizing Washington's relief resources is an ambassador's declaration of disaster.

Usually, the AID mission director keeps watch on food security indicators and functions as the U.S. ambassador's closest advisor on relief and development issues. It is the mission director's responsibility to brief the ambassador about an impending complex emergency. Early warning capabilities of impending complex emergencies have been expanded by the opening of AID offices in former Communist bloc countries. At the same time, they have been seriously compromised, particularly in Africa, by closing AID missions due to budget cuts and calls for post–Cold War downsizing. The absence of an AID mission in a country inevitably reduces the force of embassy reporting on complex emergency early warning indicators.[4]

Amartya Sen and Jean Dreze have argued that democratic regimes in the developing world have a much better record of early warning of impending famines than autocratic governments because of the existence of a free press to report on food security conditions in remote areas.[5] While Marxist regimes used starvation as a deliberate strategy for destroying population groups with suspect loyalties (for example, Stalinist Russia and Mao's China), many autocratic regimes today ignore famines simply because the bureaucratic structures are reluctant to give decision-makers bad news. In other cases there is a reluctance to publicize the onset of famine because it will be seen as a tacit admission of failed agricultural and economic policies. This is particularly true where no free press exists to apply pressure on governmental decision-makers. Even if bureaucracies do not provide early warnings and there is no free press, international NGOs frequently provide U.S. embassies, AID missions, and the media with information on what is happening in the field. One way or another, ambassadors usually hear about threatening famines. Within totalitarian regimes, limited access by diplomats to remote areas meant that these emergencies took place without public notice; but with the collapse of most such regimes, this circumstance will be uncommon in the future.

If a systematic study of State Department cable traffic preceding complex humanitarian emergencies were done, this analysis undoubtedly would be confirmed. Embassies generally do not ignore warning signs, particularly since the Ethiopian famine of 1984–85 resulted in more than a million deaths and caused political commotion in Washington. Ignoring famine can be unhealthy for a diplomat's career. Beyond career considerations, ambassadors specifically and Americans generally are intellectually unaccustomed to and emotionally unprepared for the apocalyptic scenes of starvation that accompany famine, having had no historical firsthand experience with mass starvation. The smell of death in a displaced-persons camp and the sight of a dying child are unforgettable memories for anyone. Most ambassadors who witness a famine become single-mindedly focused on relieving the suffering.

Even when the warning signs are clear, however, it does not necessarily mean that there is an adequate system in place to respond. Since the Skopje earthquake of 1963, OFDA has been in charge of responding to international natural and manmade disasters. A 1992 Government

Accounting Office audit generally affirmed the quality of OFDA's work and management. However, AID was criticized in the report for not integrating disaster mitigation into the development programs of the regional bureaus and for inadequate staffing.[6] OFDA and FFP have seldom failed to respond because of inadequate funding or internal incapacity, a circumstance that may change with the executive and legislative branch cuts in AID's budget. However, external factors have on several occasions led to a poor U.S. response. In the Ethiopian famine of 1984–85, it was the leadership of AID and the Refugee Program Office of the State Department that led the fight within the Reagan administration to initiate famine response measures. Opposition was based on the National Security Council's (NSC) argument that the United States should do nothing to aid the regime of President Haile Meriam Mengistu. Here, as elsewhere, access to the field and geopolitical confusion in the State Department about national interests are two major problems that have on occasion eviscerated U.S. famine responses.

When geopolitical interests are clearly affected by an impending complex emergency, the NSC and the State Department become a strong lobby for aggressive action. In late December 1991 and early January 1992, a massive drought struck nine countries in Southern Africa, the worst in the twentieth century in that region. Twenty-two million people were at risk. AID was called repeatedly by both the National Security Council and the Africa Bureau of the Department of State about a cable that had been received from the embassy at Harare, Zimbabwe, reporting the crop failure, proposing that measures be taken to combat the drought, and requesting assistance from Washington. Beyond the clear concern of both the State Department and the NSC about the massive loss of life that the drought might cause, both offices worried that massive population movements and economic collapse would destablize national governments in the region and might thereby endanger peace agreements in Mozambique and Angola, the democratization movement in Zambia, economic liberalization in Zimbabwe, and most troubling of all, the reform movement in South Africa. These concerns were repeatedly expressed to AID by both the NSC and State Department within days of the arrival of the Harare cable.

The NSC proposed that the Second Lady, Marilyn Quayle, whose issue focus was on disaster response, travel to the region with senior AID and Department of Agriculture officials to publicize the potential dangers that the drought posed. Her visit served to reassure anxious political leaders in the region of U.S. commitments, encouraged European contributions to the drought response, and ensured that the logistics system would be in place to deliver the 2.2 million metric tons of food pledged by the United States, which provided more than 70 percent of what was ultimately delivered by all donors. Media coverage occurred after the response was well under way and so had negligible consequences. The alarm bell had been rung by embassy and AID staff in the field and by career officers in State who realized the potential havoc that a drought-turned-famine might yield and supported OFDA and FFP efforts to mobilize resources. U.S. efforts, in fact, preceded action by other donor governments and the United Nations. The disaster response was a model for how complex emergencies might be addressed in the future. The drought's geopolitical threat added sufficient weight to the humanitarian argument to give it priority among foreign policy issues.

During the Ethiopian drought of 1989–90, the State Department once again played an active role in diplomatically supporting efforts by OFDA and FFP to find mechanisms to gain access to regions caught in the middle of the civil war that might be experiencing large-scale losses of life. Prior to Mengitsu's rise to power, Ethiopia had been a staunch ally. It is the third largest country in sub-Saharan Africa and was clearly central to Washington's interests in Africa. Herman J. Cohen, assistant secretary of state for Africa, invested substantial time trying to mediate an end to the Ethiopian civil war.

When Mengistu threatened to bomb any food shipment sent through the port of Massawa in Eritrea, Cohen asked President Bush to contact President Mikhail Gorbachev to encourage Mengistu's cooperation. Gorbachev promptly intervened and the port was opened. Although from a moral perspective Cohen was deeply troubled by the potential for large-scale loss of life, the AID drought response strengthened his hand in diplomatic negotiations to end the civil war. Once again the State Department had a geopolitical interest that added weight to the humanitarian imperative.

The Kurdish intervention by the United States and coalition force members in Northern Iraq was also motivated by both humanitarian and geostrategic calculations. While it is certainly the case that the international news media covered the massive exodus of Kurds from Iraq and that the photos did affect policy-makers, these were not the only motivating factors behind the U.S. intervention. The international news media also covered the Iraqi invasion of Kuwait, but no one would seriously suggest that the Bush administration's response to Iraqi aggression had been motivated primarily by media coverage. The Bush administration's robust response took place within two weeks of the Kurdish exodus into the mountains along the Turkish border. The prospect of a million Iraqi Kurds forming semipermanent refugee camps along the border between Turkey and Iraq was undoubtedly of great concern to the Turkish government and certainly contributed to the energy of our response. Television coverage dramatized the crisis, but there were U.S. interests irrespective of the cameras. A failure to respond would have sent a message to other groups within Iraq rebelling against Saddam Hussein that the international community would abandon them if they opposed Hussein. Since promoting Hussein's demise was in Washington's interest, strengthening the resolve of groups within Iraq opposed to his government was a geopolitical calculation requiring a humanitarian response. Determining motives is a messy and imprecise business in international relations. We can only be sure of what happened and whether it fits a geostrategic construct. In the case of Kurdistan, the geostrategic implications were not particularly mysterious. The media did play a role, but to suggest that their involvement was the primary or sole motivation for U.S. intervention would be an exaggeration.

PROPOSITION II: In an area of peripheral geopolitical importance to U.S. interests where a complex humanitarian emergency threatens, AID will initiate the relief response without outside direction if there are sufficient resources available and no approvals outside the agency are required. Print and electronic media attention will be tangential or irrelevant in the initial response, but may influence sustained funding from Congress.

In a classic study of public administration in U.S. intergovernmental grant management, Jeffrey Pressman and Aaron Wildavsky point out what should be a common sense dictum: the more sequential points in a decision-making process, the less likely closure will ever be achieved given the mathematical probability of obtaining an ever-increasing number of approvals.[7] The opposite proposition is equally valid: the fewer actors involved in a decision-making or managerial process who must say "yes," the more likely speedy action will result. When OFDA and FFP make all the decisions themselves in an emergency, whether a natural disaster or complex emergency, the response is likely to be timely, absent problems with resources or security. The mission of the two offices in droughts is simple, clear, and unambiguous: reduce the death rate by early and decisive action. Failure in a famine is easily measured and tragically visible.

Responses slow or become paralyzed when access problems complicate relief efforts either because of Somali-like chaos or because food becomes a tool of war as in the Sudan. Under these circumstances, the active engagement of State and DOD becomes essential to a successful relief response, yet is not necessarily assured. Foreign Service and U.S. military officers get trained, advance their careers, and make decisions each day based on the central presumption that national interests are defined exclusively on a geopolitical or geostrategic basis. Does the United States conduct significant trade relations with the country affected by a complex emergency? Does the country host critical U.S. military bases or control shipping lanes deemed essential to the U.S. Navy? Is the country a critical ally in an unstable region?

On virtually no geopolitical or geostrategic count does Rwanda fall within a traditional definition of American national interests, and yet the AID response to displaced people and refugees was timely and vigorous. An OFDA disaster assistance response team was dispatched to Rwanda within three weeks of the beginning of the genocide in April. Conversely, the official response to the genocide itself—which would have required armed intervention by outside military forces to stop—appeared lethargic and confused and lacked any White House, Defense Department, or senior State Department commitment. President Clinton remarked that Washington could not intervene in every crisis, a clear indication that he had no intention of responding in any manner other than through relief interventions. The DOD opposed any commitment of U.S. troops and dragged its feet even on the commitment to transport and equip African troops with armored personnel carriers. Later in the crisis, the French finally did what the African troops should have been equipped to do at the beginning when the killings could have been stopped. In this particular case, the speedy AID response was marginal because deaths resulted from organized violence and not from food insecurity, exposure or disease. The relief response was a politically inexpensive way for the United States to avoid the commitment of troops or logistical support, at least until the CNN effect altered perceptions. It was not until Congress became outraged and NGOs complained loudly that the Clinton administration finally agreed to send troops to Goma, Zaire, to assist with relief (not peacekeeping) toward the end of the genocide.

In Somalia, OFDA and FFP initiated a large-scale response in January 1992. This was undertaken prior to any NSC interest in the famine and several months before the commitment of military transport to airlift food. Media coverage of the emergency did not begin in earnest until June 1992. In fact, during congressional testimony in December 1991, and in sparsely attended media briefings on Somalia in January and February 1992, OFDA unsuccessfully attempted to draw international media attention to the disaster. Sustained media coverage of the anarchy and starvation in Somalia certainly contributed mightily to the Bush administration's decision to deploy Operation Restore Hope, but that contribution postdated Washington's decision to initiate a robust relief.

In the Sudanese drought of 1990 and the East African drought of 1993, AID initiated a relief response early in each emergency without the intervention of the State Department or White House. Again, while State was not unsympathetic, it made no attempt to press AID to act. The latter simply acted on the cable reports and field assessments done by the AID mission, OFDA, and FFP. AID carried out its mandated functions. In the case of the 1993 drought the central problem was the inadequacy of the food aid resources available to AID. Food commitments made by Washington early in the crisis were of insufficient volume and required an NGO-organized campaign to encourage a larger pledge of food aid. Not only was access an issue in the case of the 1990 Sudanese drought, but abusive Sudanese government regulation of NGOs, UN agencies, and the ICRC was so repressive that relief was paralyzed. The negotiations that took place to resuscitate both the U.S. relief effort generally and access issues specifically were conducted by AID senior officers. Their actions, along with UN efforts, helped to stave off a major disaster in the northern Sudan in 1991–92.

PROPOSITION III. The government's response to a complex humanitarian emergency in an area peripheral to American geopolitical interests will provoke opposition from career officers if 1) U.S. military force is needed, 2) the UN Security Council must become engaged, or 3) U.S. diplomatic capital must be expended to rally the support of other nations in favor of intervention. The president or Congress can intervene to reverse this opposition to intervention. The electronic media can play an important role in focusing public and policy-makers' attention to the crisis.

The career services in general, as well as political appointees, AID excepted, do not see humanitarian disaster assistance as a principal objective or undergirding principle of U.S. foreign policy. Any great power with pretensions to international leadership that embodies civilized values must make some response to human suffering to show its decency.

In geostrategically sensitive areas, disaster relief takes on enhanced significance beyond charitable purposes, but it should not in the mind of many career officers be allowed, without a strategic interest, to drive American foreign policy. Humanitarian interventionism does not have a large career constituency in State or DOD.[8]

Ambassadors use disaster relief to make political statements, which give them access to their national counterparts. If an emergency is complex, U.S. ambassadors will typically become deeply involved in political and security issues because the inherent chaos dominates all agendas of an embassy. This is not the case in Washington, where other issues of geopolitical and geostrategic importance dominate the NSC. This coordinating mechanism does not deal well with multiple crises, which tend to slow down the system. There is greater potential for error with each new crisis that must be managed by the NSC. If for no other reason than to keep the NSC docket clear of more mundane issues, the foreign policy apparatus will oppose putting complex emergencies on the agenda unless other pressures (from the president, Congress, or the media) force the issue.

While usually more uninhibited than the Pentagon in the use of military force in making foreign policy, the State Department officials tend to oppose the use of U.S. troops in complex emergencies unless they see these events as intrinsically central to national interests. Senior State Department officials in meetings with AID officers opposed military intervention in Somalia, arguing that it would set an undesirable precedent. Since the Vietnam War, a debate has been raging in the Pentagon and among international security specialists and the officer corps over the role of U.S. forces in situations other than conventional war.[9] The weight of opinion among older career military officers, who tend to be conservative politically, is that troops should only be used when U.S. geostrategic interests are directly and adversely threatened. This inhibition is most pronounced when soldiers are to be employed for security purposes and weaker when they take on a logistical mandate.

Reluctance emanates from painful memories of the Vietnam War and the understandable unwillingness to risk bloodshed on anything other than direct threats to the nation's survival. Some reluctance also comes from the absence of military training and preparation for participating in peacemaking and peacekeeping operations. Perhaps more than any other reason, however, the Pentagon typically opposes humanitarian interventionism because of tight budgets, especially during a time of convulsive downsizing. There are no readily available accounts to pay for such crises as those in Somalia, Bosnia, and Rwanda. The NSC process inherently encourages consensus-building (major actors can veto an offensive option in an analysis of options for presidential review) among major bureaucratic actors. State Department and Pentagon opposition will usually doom any proposal for troop use in humanitarian emergencies so long as no other pressures are brought to bear on the decision.

Presidential decision-making is clearly affected by the foreign policy views of the person holding the office. President Bush's precedent-setting use of the military in three emergencies (in Kurdistan, Bangladesh, and Somalia) reflected his own view of America's preeminent role in the world, its responsibility (and therefore his) for international leadership, his experience with the United Nations while permanent representative to the world organization, and his memory of his visit to the Sudan during the famine of 1985.[10] The Bush administration violated national sovereignty on at least five occasions to ensure that relief commodities were delivered to those at risk (in Angola, Liberia, Iraq, Somalia, and Ethiopia), not out of any carefully fashioned doctrine but out of practical necessity if victims were to be helped.

While it is certainly conceivable that some future president might have strong views on the subject and impose a deliberately interventionist agenda, there is little incentive for candidates for the presidency to open themselves to criticism on this issue during a campaign. There is no vocal constituency for intervention, and domestic political considerations are never far away from the White House's foreign policy decisions. Losing soldiers for vague purpose, in distant countries with names most Americans cannot pronounce, is unlikely to tempt most American political figures unless they have a humanitarian commitment or are robust internationalists.

Rwanda is probably the clearest example of a crisis where only military intervention could have stopped the genocide (by providing safe havens for noncombatants). Media coverage was extensive, more accidentally than by design, as reporters were returning from coverage of President Nelson Mandela's inauguration just as the atrocities accelerated and were diverted by their editors to report on the crisis. Unlike virtually all previous complex emergencies of the past decade, the only way to save lives was to intervene militarily. Except for conversations by Vice President Gore with African leaders at the Mandela inauguration, Washington's efforts to recruit African troops were lethargic. The Clinton administration refused repeated NGO appeals for leadership to stop the genocide. When a number of African countries volunteered troops and requested airlifts to move their troops to Rwanda along with armored personnel carriers, the United States agreed but dragged its feet for four months. All of this occurred despite massive media coverage with scenes of such horror that all previous complex emergencies paled by comparison. American troops were sent to Zaire only late and then only for logistical purposes. They were withdrawn prematurely when DOD exhausted its budget and could no longer pay for the effort.[11] CNN coverage of the carnage was insufficient to force serious U.S. support for African troop intervention.

Certainly, the limited intervention in Bosnia when the United States committed Air Force assets to provide relief during the siege of Sarajevo, the assignment of a U.S. military hospital unit in support of UN operations, and the limited airstrikes against Serbian positions were in part driven by Western media coverage of the atrocities and ethnic cleansing. OFDA and FFP were providing humanitarian assistance in Bosnia from early 1992, two years before any U.S. military assets were committed for aggressive purposes.

A compelling argument can be made that the United States had an unmistakable geopolitical and geostrategic interest in containing the Bosnian conflict, and yet both Democratic and Republican presidents have been deeply resistant to the commitment of ground forces, Clinton's campaign promises to the contrary. The instability in the Balkans could draw Germany (on the side of Croatia), Russia, Bulgaria, and Greece on the side of Orthodox Serbia, and Muslim states on the side of Bosnia into an east European war. Attempts by Serbian authorities ethnically to cleanse the Albanian population in Kosovo if it turns violent could easily draw Turkey, Macedonia, and Albania into a conflict. The Balkans could once again ignite a European war, and yet European and American intervention was weak, late, confused, and indecisive despite extensive and continuing media coverage. The CNN effect in this case was clearly exaggerated.

Presidential decisions on humanitarian intervention are much easier to make in situations where the military mission involves logistical support for NGO and UN operations rather than security in a hostile environment. The greater the likelihood of casualties in a relief operation, the less likely the operation will ever see U.S. troops in the future. The Somalia intervention, while successful in achieving President Bush's limited objectives for the first six months, reinforced the disposition against interventionism after Pakistani troops were killed in June 1993 and American troops were killed in September 1994.

Media coverage of the Ethiopian famine of the mid-1980s and of the crises in Somalia, Bosnia, and Rwanda certainly played a significant role in the U.S. government's humanitarian intervention, particularly the introduction of U.S. troops to assist with the relief effort in Somalia and Rwanda. Without that coverage, the three presidents who ordered the interventions might not have known about the catastrophic circumstances in the first place, given the lengthy formal process for getting field information to the president. Even if the presidents had known about the crises, they might not have acted without public pressure generated by graphic media coverage of mass starvation. In some instances in which a president might have wanted to intervene, media coverage would have had the effect of creating public support for what might have otherwise been a publicly misunderstood or unpopular decision. There was a high level of support from the American public both for President Bush's intervention in Somalia and for the United States to remain in Somalia to finish its work after the killing of American soldiers in October 1993.

Implications for Policy

This analysis suggests that focusing attention on the decision- making apparatus of the U.S. government would probably be more productive than focusing on attempts at reforming errant media behavior, as the latter is probably not as essential a factor as conventional wisdom suggests. The CNN factor may have consequences for fundraising for NGOs and for sustained congressional funding but is not essential to early intervention except where troops for security are critically important. Even then media coverage may not be sufficient to force a robust international response.

Downsizing AID offices in developing countries vulnerable to complex emergencies may have more impact than electronic media coverage at the later stages of an emergency, when intervention may be too late. Given the unlikelihood of reversing this reduction of a most effective early warning system, AID field missions, improved training, and more careful selection of embassy disaster relief officers may be a second line of defense. Traditionally, AID officers, and, in their absence, State Department diplomats, serve in this role. In either case, it is neither a sought-after assignment nor one that advances careers in the Foreign Service. The job description of disaster relief officers should be altered to include responsibilities for complex emergencies, particularly early warning reporting to Washington. A greater premium should be placed in Foreign Service ratings on the proper performance of these duties.

The American electronic media influences public and therefore congressional opinion. But they are businesses. Profit-making imperatives are not something over which either humanitarian relief advocates or public policy-makers have much influence. Cost-cutting occasioned by corporate mergers has forced American print and electronic media in the developing world to close faster than AID field offices.

Moreover, the television medium is naturally drawn to events with a potential for striking photography, a characteristic of complex emergencies only in their later and more deadly stages. Media coverage is not a reliable or sufficient early warning system, dependent as it is on visual images to capture editors' attention and public imagination. By the time these scenes are sufficiently dramatic to attract attention, the time for intervention has usually passed. It takes at least three to four months between the time bulk food assistance is ordered and the time it arrives in the affected area. There is a certain point in the process of starvation when people are so weakened that therapeutic interventions are ineffective. This point in time roughly corresponds to the time graphic photographs of mass starvation appear on the evening news. In the case of the famine in Ethiopia, death rates in the camps for displaced persons had begun to fall before any donor food aid began to arrive: most of the people who were at risk of dying (by some estimates 1 million people) had already died.

American media coverage of complex emergencies will likely continue to be limited, random, and unreliable. An early warning system based on the media would be costly, with no profitable consequence for investors, particularly if early warning were not successful in avoiding calamity. The international media presence in the field is simply not sufficient to provide the early warning needed to alert international opinion in a timely fashion. We can increasingly look to indigenous media in newly democratized societies to help provide early warnings, but not reliably or universally. Indeed, any survey of the developing world will readily show that the countries most at risk of falling into complex emergencies are also the least likely to have a free and developed press. Even if indigenous media were to cover a looming famine, there would be no guarantee of parallel reporting in Western countries with the resources to intervene.

Media coverage of most emergencies has been so inaccurate or so superficial that it has in some cases encouraged counterproductive responses. With a few exceptions, many reporters covering events have had little previous experience in reporting on emergencies. During the Kurdish emergencies, the *Washington Post* reported on epidemics that were not occurring and failed to report on those that were. Pressure was directed against OFDA for not responding to a meningitis epidemic in the Kurdish refugee camps when, in fact, a cholera epidemic had broken out, which required clean water and oral dehydration salts rather than medication. As a result of media criticism, the U.S. military conducted a mass inoculation campaign on all adults, which was inappropriate by OFDA and Centers for Disease Control doctrine because it reduces adults' natural immunity (mass inoculations are appropriate for children only).

The organizational location of the emergency response offices of the U.S. government affects response time and the extent to which the geopolitical designs of the State Department influence the work of OFDA and Food for Peace. Proposals to place these offices in State will quickly end the long and distinguished tradition of American leadership in complex emergencies. The ponderous clearance process of the State Department and its habit of politicizing most of what it administers will prove deadly.

We need to redefine national interests in the post–Cold War world to include complex emergencies even when there are no geostrategic interests involved. This redefinition will come only from a national debate on the role of the United States in the world, similar to the debate that took place in the immediate aftermath of World War II. We are in danger of repeating the failure of American leadership that occurred at the conclusion of World War I. After having proposed the creation of the League of Nations, President Woodrow Wilson was unable to convince the American public, or perhaps more precisely, Congress, to assume the mantle of international leadership that was available as a result of the war. It is perhaps a function of the absence of an overwhelmingly apparent menace, like the Soviet Union, that has encouraged lethargic American leadership. When the career service in DOD and State internalizes an expanded definition of national interest that includes humanitarian action, the U.S. government response to complex humanitarian emergencies will be consistently carried out in a timely and robust manner.

There is no substitute for political will in the conduct of American foreign policy, which can only be manifested through presidential leadership. While the Bush administration did not establish any notable doctrine on humanitarian intervention, its operational responses to complex emergencies established a number of important precedents for the limits of sovereignty, the use of diplomacy in support of relief operations, and military intervention—precedents with which the Clinton administration is now uncomfortably living. The Clinton presidency is entirely focused on domestic issues, except for international trade (for example, NAFTA and GATT) and foreign crises that affect domestic politics (for example, in Haiti and Mexico). President Clinton's State of the Union Address for 1995 will be remembered for its extraordinary general length and astonishing brevity on foreign affairs. By any measure it contained more limited guidance on the views of a sitting president on the state of the world than any address of its kind in the post–World War II period.

Neither media pressure nor clever administrative innovation can substitute for consistent presidential leadership in complex emergencies. While the president may not hear about complex emergencies until they are well along in their deadly slide toward chaos, presidents set foreign policy tone and by it send subtle messages to career officers and political appointees alike on what sorts of initiatives the White House will tolerate. President Clinton wants to take few foreign risks, blaze no new foreign policy paths, and focus public attention, to the extent he has influence over it, on domestic affairs. His message is not lost on the career staff of the foreign policy apparatus: take little initiative, avoid commitments, and step back from international leadership. Pressure from the media may force the president into tactical initiatives in a catastrophe, such as the Rwandan refugees at Goma, or eventually in Bosnia, but it cannot substitute for an American commitment to international leadership in complex emergencies more generally.

American leadership need not mean the commitment of U.S. troops or public foreign policy pronouncements. Demarches by the State Department as part of a governmental response to an emergency do not necessarily have to make their way into the media. If the demarches are successful, American troops may not be needed in all instances. What is more likely is that U.S. military airlift capacity, equipment, and logistical skills will be needed to support military intervention by regional powers.

In the case of a weak foreign policy presidency, the most that can be expected is that the career bureaucracy will continue to act in the manner anticipated in Propositions I and II. In the case of a geopolitically sensitive area where political and military interventions are needed for effective responses, the career officers will probably act as they would customarily. When a relief response alone is sufficient without military or diplomatic support, OFDA and Food for Peace will do their jobs. What is critical to this latter proposition is that the offices retain sufficient independence to act, and that is best done outside the State Department. When military and diplomatic support is needed, the mobilization of the electronic media to cover a complex emergency, as defined in Proposition III, may be the only way in which a distracted president can be forced to respond to a complex emergency where a large number of lives are at risk. The media's influence may be necessary but insufficient.

Notes

1. Jonathan Benthall, *Disasters, Relief and the Media* (London, 1993).

2. *Annual Report of Office of Foreign Disaster Assistance* (Washington, D.C., 1993), 46–57.

3. Internal OFDA study by Faye Henderson of the LAI/OFDA staff, August 3, 1992, for the author, then serving as assistant administrator FHA/USAID, Bureau of Food and Humanitarian Assistance.

4. Since these operating expenses have no constituency outside the agency, it is unlikely these office closings will be reversed.

5. Amartya Sen and Jean Dreze, *Hunger and Public Action* (Oxford, 1992).

6. General Accounting Office, *Foreign Disaster Assistance: AID Has Been Responsive, But Improvements Can Be Made* (October 1992).

7. Jeffrey Pressman and Aaron Wildavsky, *Implementation* (Berkeley, Calif., 1979), 105–08, 147.

8. I base this observation on my own experience with State and DOD officers during my service in the Bush administration as director of OFDA and then as assistant administrator of the Bureau of Food and Humanitarian Assistance.

9. I was activated as a Army Reserve Civil Affairs officer for three months in early 1993 to serve in the policy and plans office of the Joint Chiefs of Staff to work primarily on Somalia and Bosnia. There are certainly exceptions to this generalization. Some elements of the military do support the use of the military in complex

emergencies. It is obvious that these elements, though not the predominant opinion, are winning tactical policy battles better to prepare the U.S. military for its role in complex emergencies. Certainly the Civil Affairs branch of the army, in which I served as a reserve officer for twenty-three years, strongly supports this expansive use of the military. More than any other U.S. government bureaucracy, the U.S. military has a visceral distaste for being called to duties for which it is unprepared, as was the case in Somalia, Bosnia, and Rwanda. It is accommodating itself to its possible deployment in future emergencies despite mixed presidential signals and reservations among the officer corps about the appropriateness of this role for the military.

10. I sat through a discussion in December 1992 between President Bush and Phil Johnson, president of CARE, who was then acting as the UN director of humanitarian operations in Somalia, in which President Bush described his visit with the First Lady and Johnston to a CARE feeding center for starving children in the middle of the Sahelian famine in the mid-1980s in the Sudan. He said that he and his wife would never forget the scenes of death he witnessed then, a memory he said had clearly affected his decision to send troops into Somalia.

CHAPTER EIGHT

Human Rights and Humanitarian Crises:
Policy-Making and the Media

John Shattuck

HAVE HUMAN RIGHTS and humanitarian crises changed in the post–Cold War world? During the Cold War, threats to human rights were seen as coming largely from centralized authorities—strong governments ruling with an iron hand. The human rights community, for its part, developed the forms of advocacy with which we are now familiar—monitoring, reporting, publicizing cases, advocacy on behalf of individual victims of human rights abuse, and advocacy of sanctions against strongly abusive governments.

In the post–Cold War world, almost everything has changed. We still have the familiar paradigm of human rights abuse by strong central governments, like that of the People's Republic of China, but we have become increasingly familiar with abuses resulting from weak governments and failed states and from ethnic and religious conflicts, fanned by cynical political leaders and made worse by enormous economic, environmental, and demographic pressures. Rwanda and Bosnia are the worst examples, but there are many others as well—the Sudan, Angola, Algeria, Iraq, southeastern Turkey, East Timor, and others. These post–Cold War conflicts demand a whole new set of responses.

We start with some major new assets. The most important is a powerful new global movement for human rights and democratic participation. In the past five years this movement has changed the political face of many parts of the world, from the former Soviet Union and Eastern

Europe to South Africa, Malawi, Mongolia, Cambodia, El Salvador, and Chile. It is even beginning to show strength in unlikely places like Indonesia, Burma, and China. As evidenced at the 1993 UN World Conference on Human Rights in Vienna, the global movement for human rights and democracy is perhaps the strongest grassroots force in the world today.

This movement has not happened by itself. It is the result of efforts by countless brave men and women, working at great risk in their own countries—people like Aung San Suu Kyi in Burma, Wei Jingsheng in China, and Monsour Kikiya in Libya. Their courage is similar to the courage of great human rights leaders like Nelson Mandela, Andrei Sakharov, and Vaclav Havel, who have guided their societies to freedom in recent years. Around the world, increasingly assertive and effective indigenous forces led by people like them are pressing for greater government transparency and accountability, for basic democratic freedoms, and for internationally recognized human rights.

All this change is taking place in a new multipolar world in which states are drawn into relations with one another on a growing range of issues that transcend national borders—the expanding free market, the environment, security, population, migration—issues that are creating powerful forces of integration at some levels and increasing conflicts at others.

In this new multipolar world, the traditional human rights "sticks" of sanctions and other punitive measures directed against abusive regimes still have a role to play. But sanctions need to be complemented by broader means of promoting human rights in countries that are in the midst of wrenching change and as a consequence are often engulfed in internal conflict.

In the Cold War approach to U.S. security, threats were defined as primarily external, and the operative doctrine was containment. This focus in turn led us to direct our attention primarily to political elites and their ability to stave off those external threats—which in turn resulted in substantial U.S. assistance to authoritarian regimes and many nondemocracies.

For security reasons, foreign aid and alliances were aimed at creating strong central governments, and support for democracy was often linked to support for counterinsurgency, with a heavy cost to human rights (efforts in Central America, El Salvador, Nicaragua, and Guatemala were examples).

Since the passing of the Cold War, a very different strategic environment has emerged. External threats are now less significant than *internal* ones, such as ethnic tension, breakdown of authority, environmental destruction, refugee migrations, and so on. The focus is less on shoring up political elites, who are often the problem, and more on supporting grassroots movements for change.

A growing emphasis is now being placed on multilateral action to support these movements through a variety of means. First, there are more negotiated settlements of conflict (for example, in Central America, Cambodia, and South Africa). Second, there are more institutions of accountability for human rights abuses (for example, war crimes tribunals, truth commissions, and justice assistance programs). Third, there are more peacekeeping operations and humanitarian assistance programs (scores of UN and UN High Commissioner for Refugees operations). These are the new instruments of human rights protection.

When these instruments are applied to the human rights crises of our time—in Somalia, Bosnia, Haiti, and Rwanda—an emerging set of common humanitarian and political problems becomes evident. On the humanitarian side are enormous demands for refugee assistance, hunger relief, and other tasks to alleviate basic human suffering. But it is becoming increasingly clear that humanitarian efforts are doomed to fail unless they are accompanied by political efforts aimed at keeping the peace, establishing accountability, and deterring conflict in the long term. One of the greatest tasks facing the international community today is to create institutional mechanisms to respond to this combined and growing pressure of humanitarian and political human rights crises.

We have seen both success and failure. In the case of Haiti, the United States created an international consensus to bring about an end to thousands of killings, rapes, incidents of torture, and other human rights abuses. We also kept the pressure on the de facto regime and steadily supported the legitimacy of President Jean-Bertrand Aristide. Since his return to power, he has been helping the Haitian people to build new institutions of accountable government where none had ever existed before. He has led the liberation of millions from the worst political repression in the Western Hemisphere.

In Bosnia and Rwanda, however, there has not yet been an adequate response to the massive genocide and human rights and humanitarian catastrophes in those two countries. The situation in Bosnia is the most intractable crisis of our time. No words can express the frustration of a human rights advocate and policy-maker at the inability of the international community to bring an end to this crisis. What is being done about it?

The United States is working through the UN Security Council, where we have maintained one of the most stringent sanctions regimes in history against Serbia. We are also working to impose additional economic pressure on the Bosnian Serbs who are responsible for ongoing devastating ethnic cleansing throughout northern Bosnia. We have brought together the Bosnian government and the Bosnian Croat minority to form a federation that has helped end the fighting in central Bosnia and has reopened humanitarian convoy routes.

Moreover, the United States is working with the Europeans and the Russians for a negotiated settlement among the parties. We have provided the largest quantity of humanitarian assistance to the region and the largest in our history. Most importantly, we have led the drive to establish a War Crimes Tribunal to prosecute those responsible for genocide and crimes against humanity, have contributed $28 million so far to setting up the tribunal—more than all other counties combined—and have made clear that the tribunal is nonnegotiable in the effort to bring about peace.

But the fighting goes on, and only the most optimistic observer would say that significant improvements are in sight. Frustrations are numerous, and solutions are few. But even graver dangers lie ahead if simplistic solutions such as lifting the arms embargo are employed. The nature of the problems we face—which defy traditional borders, bend familiar notions of national interest, and do not lend themselves to diplomatic exchange—demands the sort of response that can only be put forth multilaterally, with strong leadership from the United States.

Like Bosnia, Rwanda presents all of the issues that constitute the challenge of humanitarian politics. In some ways Rwanda is a new world paradigm in which the containment of chaos is the most urgent task facing the international community. There are five stark challenges:
— alleviating the overwhelming humanitarian need for food and shelter;
— reconstituting a failed state;
— instituting accountability for genocide and crimes against humanity;
— encouraging peacekeeping among warring groups and providing security to encourage the return of refugees; and
— initiating long-term conflict resolution and preventive diplomacy to bring about a return of stability to a deeply unstable region.

How are these challenges being addressed? First, we have established war crimes tribunals. The Rwanda Tribunal was established in November 1994 by the Security Council, and investigative teams have begun to compile the evidence that will lead to indictments.

Second, we have deployed a large force of UN monitors whose work and presence can begin to promote stability and accountability. This is a key role for the UN High Commissioner for Human Rights, and the High Commissioner's success in fielding monitors will help define his new responsibilities.

Third, we must strengthen the UN peacekeeping operation in Rwanda and coordinate this operation with the humanitarian relief and human rights monitoring and enforcement activities so that the refugee camps and Rwanda itself can be made secure.

Fourth, through the UN we must assist the Rwandan government to build national institutions of justice and democracy. The United States has pledged $12 million in initial support to help rebuild the Rwandan justice system and has taken the lead in convening a twelve-nation emergency support group to provide additional assistance expertise.

Fifth, we must continue our humanitarian assistance, which now totals nearly $400 million, about 40 percent of total commitments.

Sixth, I believe the tragedy of Rwanda should stimulate expedited consideration of an International Criminal Court. While there are many differences of opinion on how to address this subject, including concerns raised by the United States, Rwanda and Bosnia clearly symbolize the compelling and urgent need for broader global human rights institutions of justice and accountability.

Bureaucracy and the Media

There are major political and bureaucratic factors that militate against U.S. intervention in cases like Bosnia and Rwanda. I would identify four syndromes in particular that have limited the U.S. response to these crises.

Vietnam and Somalia syndrome (fear of losing): This can be a healthy check on our commitment but an unhealthy inhibition against advancing U.S. post–Cold War national interests in limiting conflict.

Interagency syndrome (gridlock at the National Security Council): Interagency processes emphasize consensus, thus giving any major player (for example, the Department of Defense) an effective veto power over humanitarian intervention.

Presidential leadership syndrome: The president is not likely to take the politically risky step of intervening in a humanitarian crisis—especially if loss of life of U.S. forces is possible—unless there is strong public support for intervention.

Public support syndrome: Strong public support is unlikely until the president has stimulated it by cogently explaining that the redefinition of U.S. national interests includes the prevention of human rights and humanitarian disasters that might destabilize the world. This is a catch-22 situation, since the lack of presidential leadership and lack of public support tend to cancel each other out.

What role do the media play? The media are both the cause and effect of these new foreign policy challenges. They act as a cause in that they bring human suffering into our living rooms every hour and drive domestic public opinion. The media got us into Somalia and then got us out. They act as an effect in that the media create an increasing sense of global community resulting from images and reporting that transcend national borders. From a policy-maker's perspective, the omnipresence of the media compresses reaction time for deliberation, and makes contingency planning and readiness more important.

In discussing the media, we need to keep in mind a genuine distinction between print and electronic media. Nothing compares with the sheer intimacy of television. It has the ability to grab and galvanize the viewer and compel the public to shout: *do something!* But the electronic media also have the defects of their virtues. They tend to polarize the viewing audience, especially when the subject is Rwanda or Bosnia, initially capturing attention by eliciting outrage but steadily numbing the viewer over time through compassion fatigue.

The electronic media also have difficulty conveying the history and texture of human rights crises. Think of the pictures of Israeli soldiers shooting Palestinians. They convey no sense of what the Israelis were doing or why they were unable to leave. They convey no sense of the peace process that was unfolding as the shooting continued.

By contrast, while the print media lack the intimacy of television, they can stimulate debate because print is a medium especially well suited to convey context and meaning and to explore ranges of options. In the post–Cold War era it has largely been print articles that have set the agenda for serious policy discussion and fundamental changes in public thinking.

In our world the media are inescapable. The media are also morally neutral—their value will be determined by the uses to which they are put. One important use is to educate the public on the new global challenges of human rights and humanitarian crises like those in Bosnia, Rwanda, and Haiti—to convey an appreciation of the need to meet those challenges and to explain why meeting them is in the national interest. But the media cannot do any of that by themselves; that is the role of political leadership.

Four aspects of the political situation in the United States present growing dangers to the ability of the United States to address humanitarian crises. There is the political danger that the United States could return to an era when human rights were defined by ideology, not by facts and international standards. U.S. support for multilateral institutions like the UN could be weakened by political opponents at home at the very time when those institutions need to be strengthened most.

In addition, a new wave of domestic isolationism in the United States could overwhelm the country's human rights policy and cripple its efforts to engage with other countries in responding to human rights catastrophes. Domestic pressures to define U.S. post–Cold War national interests in economic and commercial terms could become so great that there would be no room for a strong commitment to an effective human rights policy. Those who are committed to a strong human rights policy might fail to build a domestic constituency for what we are trying to do. To put it more bluntly, the community represented by humanitarian agencies and the media might fail to explain why efforts to promote human rights accountability and enforcement in places like Rwanda should matter to American voters and taxpayers.

Part Four

CONCLUSIONS

CHAPTER NINE

Coping with the New World Disorder:
The Media, Humanitarians, and Policy-Makers

Robert I. Rotberg and Thomas G. Weiss

THE PEACE OF THE WORLD, the reduction of ethnic and religious hostilities, and the avoidance of recurring complex humanitarian emergencies depend upon a reconceptualization of American self-interest. The new sense of the national interest needs to emphasize humanitarian core values. It should elevate the freedom of peoples around the globe to the same heights that containing communism once reached. If the United States, as the world's lone superpower, does not assume these responsibilities, global tensions will proliferate.

We should accept the premise that the political values, moral stature, and domestic tranquillity of the United States are genuinely threatened by instability and strife wherever in the world they occur—even well beyond our usual geographical spheres of concern. Genocide cannot be ignored, even if the peoples being attacked are distant and their countries confer little strategic advantage. As a nation we no longer have the luxury of retreating from the world or of choosing involvements with Europe, Russia, and Israel over being engaged elsewhere and everywhere. The global village, tied together by the media and populated in part by American and international relief agencies, is a reality.

Communications have indeed become instantaneous. Mass killings anywhere appear on CNN and television news programs. A prospective genocide in Burundi, therefore, does impinge upon our own enjoyment of American freedom just as the abridgement of human rights in, say,

Burma threatens our own assertion of the universality of core moral values. Both our morality and our stability as a nation are less than fully assured when vast numbers of people around the globe are malnourished, afflicted with AIDS and malaria, poorly educated, and unfree.

The media and humanitarian NGOs have major roles to play in raising issues that will help define the national interest and in helping shape the resultant debate. Andrew Natsios indeed argues that a redefinition of the American national interest to include humanitarian involvement "will only come from a national debate on the role of the United States in the world, similar to the debate that took place in the immediate aftermath of World War II." John Shattuck sees Rwanda as "a new world paradigm, in which the containment of chaos is the most urgent task facing the international community." He urges a redefinition to include an active U.S. leadership in humanitarian crises even where geostrategic considerations are absent.

By the crises that they cover, and the depth of that coverage, the media reinforce (as in Somalia and Haiti) inherent American parochialism or expand American sensibilities, as in Rwanda, Burundi, and South Africa. Yet, as so many of the contributors to this book explain, the understanding by much of television and some of the press of what the media do wittingly and unwittingly to inform and to misinform the American public is primitive and unreflective. This book, and the meeting that laid the groundwork for the book, calls for a greater self-consciousness on the part of the media when covering (usually) unfamiliar kinds of crises in unfamiliar locales. It calls for a greater awareness on the part of human-itarian organizations. It further urges new kinds of cooperation between the media and the humanitarians in the field and at home.

The chapters in this book have discussed how the media and humani-tarians do and should behave in the field, how that interaction can be fur-thered and improved, and the extent to which the media and humanitarians can both influence the making of well-informed and well-considered policy toward future complex humanitarian emergencies, ethnic and reli-gious conflicts, incipient genocide, and other tragedies. Of the many wise observations and suggestions in the chapters, eight seem unusually salient.

Public Opinion, Elusive Yet Indispensable

What is the influence of public opinion on foreign policy-making in general and on humanitarian crises in particular? There is little consensus beyond an agreement that ignoring the subject would have negative consequences for an ever-growing number of victims. As with the media, public opinion should be disaggregated into its different constituent components to reflect the different receptivities of each.

At one end of the spectrum, the public is receptive. There is evidence that the public is interested if it can relate humanitarian crises to everyday life and to the welfare of the country as a whole. At the other end of the spectrum is a skepticism that the American public wants to help but is unwilling to commit the resources necessary to prevent or contain humanitarian crises. There is a "popular ambivalence" about the utility of assisting what is frequently portrayed, in Fred Cate's view, as a corrupt and hopeless Third World. This skepticism is exacerbated by public doubts about whether current developments in the Third World are necessarily good for U.S. interests. There is a residue in the public's eyes, if not in the eyes of scholarly and more popular analysts of interdependence, of zero-sum global competition among states. As a result, the public sometimes appears suspicious of "giveaway" agendas, fearing that precious tax dollars will be wasted. Presidential leadership is required, as in the case of Haiti, to turn public opinion from its traditional "charity starts at home" attitude to a support of humanitarian efforts overseas. As both Natsios and Shattuck note, there is no substitute for leadership from the Oval Office.

The limited attention span of American readers, viewers, or listeners contrasts with that of Dutch and Scandinavian counterparts, for instance, and may reflect the high costs of foreign news coverage. Journalists may thus attempt on occasion to be "missionaries," seeking when possible to override the commercial concerns of proprietors and editors. However, if media coverage of humanitarian crises exceeds public interest, it may thus be best to anticipate and exploit temporary surges of public interest and to inform the public steadily, rather than to assume a continuous public awareness.

Competition and Cooperation

Should the media have a humanitarian agenda? Or should the media be morally neutral, and simply report what they see? News of humanitarian import competes legitimately for attention with business, sports, and entertainment. Although the media have an indispensable impact in the humanitarian sphere, they cannot be harnessed to a humanitarian mission pure and simple. News related to humanitarian issues quite properly competes for attention with business, sports, and entertainment news—what critics wryly but too dismissively describe as "info-tainment." Hence, the media and humanitarians have roles to play in informing the public, but there is no substitute for political leadership in articulating the various national interests and values served by an active U.S. engagement in complex humanitarian crises.

Edward Girardet underlines this reality in scrutinizing the economics of the media industry. Cate examines it in determining new electronic possibilities. The media must be objective, but they can be helped to open their individual and collective eyes.

A "humanitarian correctness" test, which would inject a positive spin on events or an arbitrary balance between bad news and good news, would be unacceptable. At the same time, the media do make choices, and there is a place for a presumption of concern for all humanity. And many journalists themselves are attracted by news that solves problems and makes a difference, despite the cynicism that emanates from visible TV anchors commanding multimillion-dollar salaries. Thus, humanitarian agencies have potential collaborators who are favorably predisposed, if requiring friendly cooperation and guidance.

Motivating opinion-page columnists is also worthwhile because they fill guaranteed spaces on a regular basis. Editors are prime targets, but owners and publishers are wary of cultivation and are therefore harder to reach. Reporters are controlled by gatekeepers; however, the harsh economics of the industry mean that greater use can and should be made of stringers and local journalists. Many of the most important humanitarian stories of the decade have been broken by locally resident media persons.

Telling the Whole Story

Humanitarians are particularly keen to achieve a wider understanding of the root causes of crises. They correctly bemoan reducing complex crises to slogans like "chaos" and "anarchy." Failed states are not simply a reflection of African incompetence or corruption but can be explained by such other factors as weapons proliferation, repressive regimes, external interference, and scarcity. Media coverage of the carnage in Rwanda, for example, was essentially flawed, say Girardet, Peter Shiras, and John

Hammock and Joel Charny, insofar as the basic struggle was portrayed as one involving heroic foreign relief workers and not flawed operations, root causes, and local capacities.

Members of the electronic media exert significant pressure on government officials to "do something" in response to crises, although that "something" is rarely sufficient or sustained, as virtually all the authors agree. However, such pressure also has a potentially negative effect, stimulating outrage at first and then leading to compassion fatigue. Print media, although lacking in immediacy, are better able to convey the complexity of humanitarian issues. The print media have set the agenda for serious policy discussion and have done much to stimulate meaningful debate about humanitarian crises.

Aid agencies could well develop a cadre of media specialists. Regular briefings of the media in the field might help achieve increased in-depth coverage. At the same time, training journalists to be knowledgeable about humanitarian issues could undoubtedly be done—even though media professionals scoff at such an idea—and aid agencies could certainly open themselves up to scrutiny and be more prepared for coverage of failure and corruption among their own ranks.

Efforts to increase awareness of the causes of crises before the outbreak of violence are critical. Yet resources available for media relations are limited, given that the priority during emergencies is relief and protection. Moreover, media coverage should only build upon greater public education, which means that the burden of training and informing the media falls primarily on aid agencies. "Development education," long buzzwords in the vocabulary of NGOs, must become a priority, according to Shiras, Lionel Rosenblatt, and Hammock and Charny.

"Telling the whole story" also carries a risk for humanitarian agencies. Aid is already a political liability of sorts, especially since the 1994 congressional elections in the United States. Further scrutiny of humanitarian assistance might weaken the political and public support for that mission. Yet humanitarian agencies should still take the moral high ground of transparency and accountability.

Facilitating Access

The media require access to better and more accurate information. Critics should take positive steps to assist in providing access. Insufficient access can result from logistical or bureaucratic barriers, as Steven Livingston shows in his comparison of the noncoverage of the southern Sudan in contrast to the better visibility of other crises, including that in nearby Somalia. His chapter also discusses additional obstacles to access, such as physical safety and the interference of governments. Moreover, the ingredients of a compelling "story" (the implosion of Somalia and the evaporation of sovereignty in Rwanda are examples) should be evaluated afresh because complex emergencies necessitate a special appeal to viewers and readers to distinguish them from the globe's steady diet of bad news.

Should humanitarians help journalists and television crews cover stories in remote and dangerous locations? Should aid agencies bump aid cargo or personnel off aid flights in order to make room for news crews, often the only way in which reporters can reach the front lines of humanitarian crises? As Girardet notes, aid agencies have to weigh the relative merits of tangible assistance against potential publicity for an overlooked cause; journalists must worry about the danger of becoming "overly dependent" on the humanitarians, and, hence, "uncritical." Sharing access to conflict zones with the media may also create problems for aid agencies, whose own ability to work in these areas may be granted by political authorities or insurgent movements only on the understanding that they stay silent about conditions and causes. Working closely with the media may, consequently and unwittingly, jeopardize their fundamental missions.

Ready access to information from aid agencies is important for strengthening productive relationships with the media. Information officers or directors of aid agencies who are unwilling to meet with the media hardly facilitate such a process, as Shiras argues so persuasively. He and others also argue that humanitarian agencies should employ trained media officers in the field.

Understanding the Plurality and Complexity of the Media

A large, worldwide humanitarian agency known for its visibility and high public profile was shocked during our deliberations to learn from journalists that it was known only for its "children and Christmas cards." All agencies should develop a sophisticated and tailored strategy to engage the different types and formats of media coverage. Doing so requires influencing key gatekeepers (publishers, editors, and so on) who determine what is covered and how.

Yet the nature of news and news-gathering means that humanitarian crises invariably rise to prominence rapidly but remain on the radar screen only briefly. Aid agencies should not expect slow burning fuses like the southern Sudan to capture attention in the same way as Rwanda's genocide did in 1994. Fortunately, policy-making is not entirely driven by headlines and crises. Ongoing coverage of mostly invisible but festering emergencies also has value—in fact, it may be the critical challenge. As Hammock and Charny write, the "scripted morality play" that uses "emotion-charged pleas that depict beneficiaries as helpless and feeble" is myopic and potentially counterproductive. In fostering a change away from mere reaction to prevention, the challenge will be even greater, as Rosenblatt indicates, because in cases like Somalia and Rwanda "media coverage and military intervention were too little, too late, or too ineffectual." Humanitarians need to help the media focus on tension-filled situations before they erupt into crises.

The media are not monolithic. For example, while audience ratings have slipped, CNN remains a vehicle for reaching policy-makers who, as many remarked, may leave their televisions turned on all day in their offices as a kind of alert mechanism. Equally, national newspapers may influence the policy agenda of the elite, for example through early-bird press clippings circulated in the State Department. Regional newspapers reach a cross-section of Americans but may only report on volcanic human emergencies.

Gatekeepers prefer exclusives, which, as every journalist knows, are the ultimate seduction. At the same time, the herd instinct sometimes devalues a story not being pursued by the competition. Journalists also sounded a warning against efforts by aid agencies at spin control or exaggeration. Handouts are not stories and agencies should avoid bringing political correctness into relief coverage. As Girardet wishes and Hammock and Charny argue, "relief agencies have to be prepared for greater media scrutiny." Enhancing accountability both to funders as well as to victims for the results of relief and protection efforts is urgently required.

Hoarding information by aid agencies in an attempt to manipulate the media often breeds antagonism and cynicism. It would be preferable to train relief workers in the field to work closely with journalists rather than to post press officers to crisis sites. Ultimately, there is no substitute for helping journalists to witness unfolding events for themselves.

Realities: Understanding Media Commercialism

The growth of entertainment journalism, primarily on television, is universally recognized. This growth can reduce foreign news to a formula or squeeze it out altogether, risking the loss of broader audiences. Moreover, "the need by certain media for ever more powerful imagery" has, according to Girardet, "gone right over the top" after Rwanda and Bosnia.

Newspapers, too, are under increasing commercial pressure. Price hikes in the United States of over 30 percent for newsprint in 1995 have reduced news openings for international news even further. The current newspaper format has been described as "a device to deliver consumers to producers." In other words, finely tuned advertising was viewed as already having effectively driven layout and editorial decisions. By way of contrast, the *Boston Globe,* one of New England's major newspapers, during the last two decades has reversed the classic supply-to-demand equation by educating its public to develop a taste for foreign news.

New Technology, Old Problems

Major features of the information explosion (in Cate's view, particularly advances in television news-gathering, the spread of the Internet, and the increase in interactive communications) raise as many issues as they resolve. These include access, management, cost, and impact on policy and public opinion. More information does not necessarily bring greater knowledge. Junk mail remains a problem as it expands from the mailbox to the fax machine and e-mail. Indeed, the broader spectrum of available news sources may oblige humanitarian groups to adopt an ever more diverse strategy to promote their messages.

Journalists, like everyone else, must sort through the information that swamps them. Technology does not necessarily breed trust, the human contact so valued by journalists. "Don't send me faxes," said one journalist, who still sorts out his mountain of incoming communications, postal or electronic, by looking for a familiar name or contact.

All three sets of actors—the media, policy-makers, and humanitarians—need to develop strong working relationships, which can best be based on trust built up over an extended period of time. As a result of having established working relationships, some journalists, simply because they trust a source, confidently proceed with stories where corroboration is otherwise time consuming or impossible. Rosenblatt, for example, provided advance but unverifiable information in Bosnia, which led to a dramatic and decisive story and policy changes of the type that he had sought.

Technology is not the primary constraint working against more timely and more effective humanitarian action. Policy analysts have an awesome capability to be forewarned of and to track crises. But that leaves us with the "what for?" How to mobilize adequate political support in order to respond to warnings of developing crises still remains the most crucial of questions with the least obvious of answers, as Natsios notes throughout his chapter.

Would interactive information and news services reduce the power of the traditional gatekeepers, whom Livingston's theory and quantitative analyses point to as a primary drag on more and better humanitarian coverage? These interactive capabilities might change the way in which the gatekeepers worked. However, many participants doubted the ability of gatekeepers to manage the amount of information available. Yet the effects of the new technology in poorer parts of the world could be liberating, especially as populations struggle to achieve basic literacy.

Focusing on the Policy Process

Despite differences of opinion on the precise degree of the media's impact on policy, the policy context is much wider than the TV screen. In other words, the U.S. government responds to crises for reasons other than nonstop coverage on CNN. Considerable policy-making goes on at lower bureaucratic levels, immune from media influences, as both Rosenblatt and Natsios maintain.

There is an increasingly bureaucratic resistance to disaster relief in complex crises, especially in relation to the degree of involvement by outside military forces. Much of this resistance is a result of the Somalia syndrome, even though the media originally contributed to propelling policy beyond natural caution. When no geostrategic interests are at stake in a particular humanitarian emergency and involvement poses real danger for military and humanitarian personnel, such resistance may be increasingly difficult to overcome. Presidential Decision Directive (PDD) 25 was issued in May 1994 and proved yet another constraint in Rwanda, in spite of what everyone inside and outside of government agreed was genocide. Probably more than other world defense ministries, the Pentagon in 1995 is torn between assuming humanitarian duties in order to preserve its budget and refusing to assume nontraditional functions that may undercut military readiness.

There are three uses for the media in the policy process. First, the media may be employed to project messages within the bureaucracy. A news story can be a "super interoffice memo." Second, the media may be used to set an agenda. For example, the media, carefully briefed, helped launch a controversial change in food aid policy during the Somalia crisis. Third, the media may be used to build a constituency for action. Cases include the media coverage of the Kurdish refugee crisis in northern Iraq and the coverage that generated pressure for U.S. military assistance in Rwanda. Even in a case-by-case approach keyed to identifying specific U.S. interests directly affected by this or that emergency, the defense of international norms should play a role. An international system in which genocide is not a policy option would be in U.S. interests, just as one would be in which war criminals would at least hesitate before resorting to ethnic cleansing.

We recommend that:

— The media should become more knowledgeable about humanitarian issues and exercise independent judgment with regard to them rather than rely on information supplied by warring factions, the UN, NGOs, donor governments, or other parties interested in the process. They should go beyond simplistic formulas, often reinforced by the perceived need to mimic competitors, and delve deeply into the meaning of crises.

— Journalists should encourage editors, publishers, and owners to extend coverage of humanitarian issues both to unreported crises and beyond the short sharp peaks of most crisis reporting.

— International media should do more to support local media institutions and journalists.

— Responsible journalism should entail a commitment to take readers and viewers beyond their immediate self-interest: to lead as well as reflect public opinion.

— Aid organizations should develop sophisticated communications strategies that take account of the plurality and complex nature of the media industry and of the possibilities of new technologies. They should not assume that other actors are aware of their objectives and programs.

— Coalitions or informal groupings of organizations should be used to maximize resources, especially in developing improved communications strategies.

—Specialist targeting of materials and other niche marketing skills should be employed. Organizations should not rely exclusively on traditional methods of publicity, like press conferences and releases, but also employ individual and specialist contacts and an array of emerging electronic possibilities.

—During crises, organizations should balance the need for opportunism with a long-term commitment to explaining root causes.

—Policy-makers should not let the media or humanitarian organizations set or preempt the agenda. Time and resources spent in educating the public over the long term will help reduce the problems of managing public opinion in crises. More public resources should be channeled to education and advocacy efforts by non-governmental organizations.

About the Authors

Fred H. Cate is an associate professor of law and faculty advisor to the *Federal Communications Law Journal*, at the Indiana University School of Law, Bloomington. He is also senior fellow of The Annenberg Washington Program in Communication Policy Studies. He edited *International Disaster Communications: Harnessing the Power of Communications to Avert Disasters and Save Lives* (Washington, D.C., 1994), and is the author of *Media, Disaster Relief and Images of the Developing World* (Washington, D.C., 1994).

Joel R. Charny is policy director of Oxfam America, a private, non-profit international agency that funds self-help development in poor nations in Africa, Asia, Latin America, and the Caribbean. He has been working with Oxfam America since 1980, serving as Southeast Asia projects officer, Asia regional director, and overseas director. Charny has written extensively on relief and development issues, especially those related to Asia. His opinion pieces have appeared in a number of major newspapers, including the *New York Times*, *Los Angeles Times*, *International Herald-Tribune*, and *Wall Street Journal*.

Edward R. Girardet has been an independent journalist and producer since 1989, covering international current events, development, and environmental issues for European and North American broadcasters. Girardet has had recent assignments with the *MacNeil-Lehrer NewsHour*, Britain's *Channel Four*, and various European networks, with documentary and magazine segments in the Middle East, Africa, Europe, and the Caribbean. He edits *CROSSLINES Global Report*, a Geneva-based independent news journal on humanitarian action, development, and global issues. Girardet has received numerous awards for his journalism, including the Sigma Delta Chi Award for distinguished reporting (1985), an Overseas Press Club citation for the best foreign coverage (1987), and a Freedom House Award for distinguished reporting. He is editing a book on media and war in Somalia and Rwanda.

John C. Hammock is a fellow at the Center for Hunger, Poverty, and Nutrition Policy of Tufts University. He served as president of Oxfam America from 1984 to 1995. An expert on economic and community development in the global South, Hammock also served as executive director of Accion International, which provides technical assistance to self-help enterprises in South America and the Caribbean.

Steven Livingston is assistant professor of political communication and international affairs at George Washington University. His interests concern the media and politics, particularly relating to international affairs and U.S. foreign policy. He focuses on campaigns and elections, especially concerning the role of the mass media, voting behavior, public opinion, and political socialization. He wrote *The Terrorism Spectacle: The Politics of Terrorism and the News Media* (Boulder, Colo., 1994).

Andrew Natsios is vice president of World/Vision, where he is responsible for program development, evaluation, and resource acquisition for relief and development programs in developing countries, the Commonwealth of Independent States, and Eastern Europe. Previously, he was assistant administrator for the Bureau of Food and Humanitarian Assistance at USAID and director of the Office of its Foreign Disaster Assistance. He has also been active in local and state politics, serving in the local government of Holliston, Massachusetts, and as a state representative. Natsios has served in the U.S. Army Reserves since 1972 and is a veteran of the Gulf War. He served on the Joint Staff at the Pentagon on active duty in 1993, working on issues facing Somalia and Bosnia.

Lionel Rosenblatt is president of Refugees International. Under his direction, Refugees International has expanded from its initial focus on Indochinese refugee issues to life-threatening refugee crises around the world. Earlier, as a foreign service officer, Rosenblatt served in Sri Lanka, Vietnam, and Thailand. He was founder and chief of the Refugee Section at the U.S. Embassy in Bangkok (1975-1976) and later served as refugee coordinator and director of the Khmer Emergency Group during the 1978–81 crisis. Rosenblatt was director of the Office of Special Concerns, Interagency Task Force for Indochinese Refugees at the State Department, laying fundamental groundwork for the Southeast Asian Refugee program.

Robert I. Rotberg is president of the World Peace Foundation. He also is a research associate at the Harvard Institute for International Development and teaches third world politics at the Kennedy School of Government. Rotberg was professor of political science and history at the Massachusetts Institute of Technology (1968–87) and became academic vice president of Tufts University and president of Lafayette College before returning to Cambridge. He is the author of more than two dozen books and numerous articles on the politics of Africa, especially South Africa, and on the politics of Haiti.

John Shattuck is assistant secretary of state for democracy, human rights and labor. He formerly was vice president for government, community and public affairs of Harvard University, a lecturer at the Harvard Law School, and executive director of the Washington office of the American Civil Liberties Union.

Peter Shiras is director of government relations and public outreach for InterAction, a coalition of more than 150 U.S.-based relief and development organizations. Prior to joining InterAction, he served for thirteen years in various capacities for the Catholic Relief Services, most recently as director for public policy liaison and senior director for Africa. Before coming to Catholic Relief Services, Shiras was an agricultural economist for several organizations, including the Inter-American Development Bank, the Institute of Agricultural Sciences and Technology of the Guatemalan Ministry of Agriculture, and Oxfam (U.K.). He has published numerous articles in the *New York Times*, the *Washington Post*, and elsewhere.

Thomas G. Weiss is associate director of Brown University's Watson Institute for International Studies and executive director of the Academic Council on the United Nations System. Previously he held several UN posts (at UNCTAD, the UN Commission for Namibia, UNITAR, and ILO). Weiss also served as executive director of the International Peace Academy. He has written extensively on aspects of development, peace-keeping, humanitarian relief, and international organizations. His most recent books are *NGOs, the UN, and Global Governance* (Boulder, Colo., 1996), with Leon Gordenker; *The United Nations and Civil Wars* (Boulder, Colo., 1995); *Mercy Under Fire* (Boulder, Colo., 1995), with Larry Minear; and *The United Nations and Changing World Politics* (Boulder, Colo., 1994), with David Forsythe and Roger Coate.

About the Sponsoring
Institutions

The World Peace Foundation

The World Peace Foundation was created in 1910 by the imagination and fortune of Edwin Ginn, the Boston publisher, to encourage international peace and cooperation. The Foundation seeks to advance the cause of world peace through study, analysis, and the advocacy of wise action. As an operating, not a grant-giving foundation, it provides financial support only for projects which it initiates itself.

Edwin Ginn shared the hope of many of his contemporaries that permanent peace could be achieved. That dream was denied by the outbreak of World War I, but the Foundation has continued to attempt to overcome obstacles to international peace and cooperation, drawing for its funding on the endowment bequeathed by the founder. In its early years, the Foundation focused its attention on building the peacekeeping capacity of the League of Nations and then on the development of world order through the United Nations. The Foundation established and nurtured the premier scholarly journal in its field, *International Organization*, now in its forty-eighth year.

From the 1950s to the early 1990s, mostly a period of bipolar conflict when universal collective security remained unattainable, the Foundation concentrated its activities on improving the working of world order mechanisms, regional security, transnational relations, and the impact of public opinion on American foreign policy. From 1980 to 1993 the Foundation published nineteen books and seven reports on Third World security; on South Africa and other states of southern Africa; on Latin America, the Caribbean, and Puerto Rico; on migration; and on the international aspects of traffic in narcotics. In 1994 and 1995, the Foundation published books on Europe after the Cold War and on the United States, southern Europe, and the countries of the Mediterranean basin.

The Foundation now focuses its energies and resources on preventing intercommunal conflict and humanitarian crises. These projects proceed from the assumption that large-scale human suffering, wherever it occurs, is a serious and continuing threat to the peace of the world, both engendering and resulting from ethnic, religious, and other intrastate and cross-border conflicts. The Foundation is examining how the forces of world order may most effectively engage in preventive diplomacy, create early warning systems leading to early preventive action, achieve regional conflict avoidance, and eradicate the underlying causes of intergroup enmity and warfare.

The Thomas J. Watson Jr. Institute for International Studies at Brown University

Brown University's Thomas J. Watson Jr. Institute for International Studies was established in 1986 to promote the work of students, faculty, visiting scholars, and policy practitioners who are committed to analyzing global problems and developing initiatives that address them. The Watson Institute promotes research, teaching, and public education on international affairs, an area of inquiry that encompasses inter-state relations; transnational, regional, and global phenomena; and cross-national, comparative studies.

The Watson Institute supports and coordinates the activities of scholars and practitioners with interdisciplinary approaches to contemporary global problems. Most are social scientists working on political, economic, social, or cultural issues, along with scholars from the humanities and the natural sciences whose perspectives contribute directly to the understanding of these issues. The Watson Institute's affiliated centers and programs currently engage in a broad range of activities, from improving the teaching of international studies to contributing to research and public education about international security, the comparative study of development, health, hunger, the United Nations, U.S. foreign policy, and issues arising within Africa, the Americas, Asia, Europe, the Middle East, and the former Soviet Union.

The Humanitarianism and War Project is a special research and applied policy effort that is supported by over thirty governments, UN organizations, non-governmental organizations, and foundations. Resulting from its firsthand research in war zones are a number of case studies, articles, and books containing relevant lessons for practitioners and conceptual insights for analysts. The role of the media in complex emergencies is an ongoing interest.

Index

197